Disclaimer

Book Title: Computer Security Division 2010 Annual Report

Book Author: Patrick D. O'Reilly;

Book Abstract: This annual report covers the work conducted within the National Institute of Standards and Technology's Computer Security Division during Fiscal Year 2010. It discusses all projects and programs within the Division, staff highlights, and publications.

Citation: NIST Interagency/Internal Report (NISTIR) - 7751

Keywords: annual report; computer security; Computer Security Division; CSD; cyber security; FISMA; highlights; projects

NIST
National Institute of
Standards and Technology
U.S. Department of Commerce

Computer Security Division

2010 Annual Report

Table of Contents

Welcome

The Computer Security Division (CSD), a component of NIST's Information Technology Laboratory (ITL), conducts research, development and outreach necessary to provide standards and guidelines, tools, metrics and practices to protect our nations information and communication infrastructure.

In fiscal year (FY) 2010, CSD continued to build on its work in security management and assurance, cryptography and systems security, identity management and emerging security technologies. CSD played a vital role in both national and international security standard setting. The division continues its leadership role in technologies and standards for Cloud Computing, Identity Management and as a Government Wide Leader and national coordinator for the National Initiative for Cybersecurity Education (NICE). In addition, this year marked the publication of NIST Interagency Report (NISTIR) 7628, *Guidelines for Smart Grid Security,* which identifies security requirements applicable to the Smart Grid, security-relevant use cases, logical interface diagrams and interface categories, vulnerability classes abstracted from other relevant cyber security documents, specific issues applicable to the Smart Grid, and privacy concerns. We also continued to provide reference specifications in multiple areas, allowing others to leverage our work to increase the security of their systems and products.

Our role as a collaborator for both government and industry is essential for the success of our mission and in FY2010 we continued to reach out to partners across the government, industry and the world. We embraced international cooperation in our SHA-3 competition as we work on a successor to our current government-approved hash algorithm. We received reviews from the international cryptographic community that allowed us to narrow down the acceptable candidates from 51 to less than seven. Being able to call on such a deep pool of international expertise will encourage acceptance of the final algorithm and surety with regards to its strength.

Industry represents a key audience and partner in all of our work. The success of the Security Content Automation Protocol (SCAP) program is dependent on our partnership with them. Industry has advised us on the need for the program and its evolution. There was enthusiastic adoption from many industry partners and their continued support has allowed us to move ahead with this program much more quickly than otherwise. As a result of such cooperation, we have created and are maintaining a significant repository of SCAP compliant security checklists for use with an ever-increasing number of security tools.

The responsibilities assigned to NIST, and by extension, CSD in the Federal Information Security Management Act (FISMA) to assist the federal agencies in securing their information systems is a major part of the work that we do. This year marked a historic point in that work with the release of Special Publication 800-37, Revision 1, *Guide for Applying the Risk Management Framework to Federal Information Systems: A Security Life Cycle Approach.* Not only was this a product of the new cooperation between NIST and the entities responsible for the security requirements for national security systems (the Department of Defense, the Director of National Intelligence and the Committee on National Security Systems), but it also presented a completely new approach for federal agencies to take to information security.

Looking forward to FY2011, CSD plans to continue its work in information security, producing standards, guidelines, technical reference materials and specifications to improve the information security management of systems across the Nation and around the world.

Donna Dodson

Chief, Computer Security Division &
Deputy Chief Cybersecurity Advisor

Division Organization

Donna Dodson
Chief, Computer Security Division &
Deputy Chief Cybersecurity Advisor

Group Managers

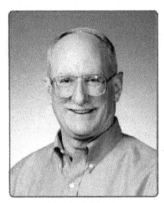

William Burr
Cryptographic Technology Group

David Ferraiolo
Systems and Emerging Technologies
Security Research Group

Matthew Scholl
Security Management and Assurance Group

The Computer Security Division Implements the Federal Information Security Management Act of 2002

The E-Government Act, Public Law 107-347, passed by the 107th Congress and signed into law by the President in December 2002, recognized the importance of information security to the economic and national security interests of the United States. Title III of the E-Government Act, entitled the Federal Information Security Management Act of 2002 (FISMA), included duties and responsibilities for the National Institute of Standards and Technology, Information Technology Laboratory, Computer Security Division (CSD). In 2010, CSD addressed its assignments through the following projects and activities:

Issued fifteen final NIST Special Publications (SP) that addressed management, operational and technical security guidance in areas such as, securing WiMax wireless networks, secure content automation protocols, protection of personally identifiable information, Bluetooth security, and deployment of Secure Domain Name System deployment. In addition, eight draft SPs were issued for public comment for cryptographic key deployment and security configuration management among other topics;

- Continued the successful collaboration with the Office of the Director of National Intelligence, Committee on National Security Systems and the Department of Defense to establish a common foundation for information security across the federal government, including a consistent process for selecting and specifying safeguards and countermeasures (i.e., security controls) for federal information systems;

- Provided assistance to agencies and private sector: Conducted ongoing, substantial reimbursable and non-reimbursable assistance support, including many outreach efforts such as the Federal Information Systems Security Educators' Association (FISSEA), the Federal Computer Security Program Managers' Forum (FCSM Forum), and the Small Business Corner;

- As part of its contribution to the Smart Grid initiative, CSD released NIST IR 7628, *Guidelines for Smart Grid Cyber Security,* in August 2010;

- Reviewed security policies and technologies from the private sector and national security systems for potential federal agency use: hosted a growing repository of federal agency security practices, public/private security practices, and security configuration checklists for IT products. Con-

tinued to lead, in conjunction with the Government of Canada's Communications Security Establishment, the Cryptographic Module Validation Program (CMVP). The Common Criteria Evaluation and Validation Scheme (CCEVS) and CMVP facilitate security testing of IT products usable by the federal government;

- Co-hosted the third annual HIPAA Security Rule conference, "Safeguarding Health Information: Building Assurance through HIPAA Security", to assist organizations in addressing security and privacy concerns in the growing use of HIT, and to discuss challenges, tips, and techniques for implementing the requirements of the HIPAA Security Rule;

- Developed conformance test procedures to ensure compliance with the HIT meaningful use security standards and certification criteria;

- Solicited recommendations of the Information Security and Privacy Advisory Board on draft standards and guide lines and solicited recommendations of the Board on information security and privacy issues regularly at quarterly meetings;

- Held a successful "SHA-3 conference" and selected five "finalist" candidate algorithms as a part of a public competition to select a new federal cryptographic hash function standard;

- Provided outreach, workshops, and briefings: Conducted ongoing awareness briefings and outreach to CSD's customer community and beyond to ensure comprehension of guidance and awareness of planned and future activities. CSD also held workshops to identify areas that the customer community wishes to be addressed, and to scope guidelines in a collaborative and open format; and

- Produced an annual report as a NIST Interagency Report (IR). The 2003-2009 Annual Reports are available via our Computer Security Resource Center (CSRC) website.

Security Management and Assurance Group

STRATEGIC GOAL

The Security Management and Assurance (SMA) Group provides leadership, expertise, outreach, validation, standards and guidelines to assist the federal IT community in protecting information and information systems, and in using these critical assets to accomplish federal agency missions.

Overview

Information security is an integral element of good management. Information and information systems are critical assets that support the mission of an organization. Protecting them can be as important as protecting other organizational resources, such as money, physical assets, or employees. In order to protect their assets, organizations need to have assurance that the security technologies that they invest in can work and allow interoperability, especially in the area of cryptography, as well as management guidance. However, including security considerations in the management of information and computers does not completely eliminate the possibility that these assets will be harmed. In order to reduce the risk to their assets, organizations need to also have assurance that the security technologies that they invest in can work and allow interoperability, especially in the area of cryptography, as well as management guidance.

Ultimately, responsibility for the success of an organization lies with its senior management. These officials establish the organization's computer security program and its overall program goals, objectives, and priorities in order to support the mission of the organization. They are also responsible for ensuring that required resources are applied to the program.

Collaboration with other organizations is critical for success. Within the federal government, we collaborate with the U.S. Office of Management and Budget (OMB), the U.S. Government Accountability Office (GAO), and all Executive Branch agencies. We also work closely with a number of information technology organizations and standards bodies, as well as with public and private organizations. Internationally we work jointly with the governments of our allies, including Canada, Japan, Australia, and several European and Asian countries, to standardize and validate the correct implementation of cryptography.

Major initiatives in this area include:

- The Federal Information Security Management Act (FISMA) Implementation project;

- The Cryptographic Module Validation Program;

- The Cryptographic Algorithm Validation Program;

- Extended outreach initiatives to federal and nonfederal agencies, state and local governments and international organizations;

- Security for Electronic Health Care Information;

- Security Standards and Conformance for the Nation's Smart Grid;

- Outreach to small and medium businesses;

- Standards development;

- The National Initiative for Cybersecurity Education; and

- Producing and updating NIST Special Publications (SP) on security management topics.

Key to the success in this area is our ability to interact with a broad constituency – federal and non-federal in order to ensure that our program is consistent with national objectives related to or impacted by information security.

Federal Information Security Management Act Implementation Project

The Federal Information Security Management Act (FISMA) of 2002 (URL: http://csrc.nist.gov/drivers/documents/FISMA-final.pdf) requires each federal agency to develop, document, and implement an agency-wide program to provide information security for the information and information systems that support the operations and assets of the agency, including those provided or managed by another agency, contractor, or other source. The FISMA Implementation Project focuses on the development and updating of the security standards and guidance required to effectively implement the provisions of the legislation. The implementation of the NIST standards and guidance helps agencies to create and maintain robust information security programs and to effectively manage risk to agency operations, agency assets, and individuals.

To support the implementation of the NIST standards and guidelines for FISMA, NIST defined the Risk Management Framework (RMF), illustrated in the figure below. The RMF provides a disciplined and structured process that integrates information security and risk management activities into the system development life cycle.

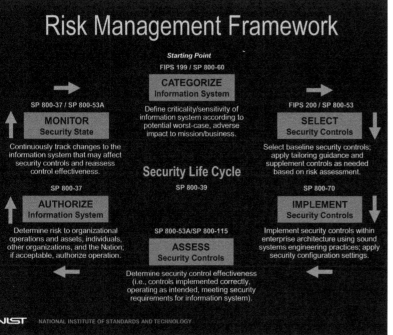

Federal Information Security Management Act Implementation Project – Phase I

CSD continued to develop the security standards and guidelines required by federal legislation. Phase I of the FISMA Implementation Project included the development of security standards and guidelines to assist federal agencies in—

- Implementing the individual steps in the NIST RMF as part of a well-defined and disciplined system development life cycle process;

- Demonstrating compliance to specific requirements contained within the FISMA legislation; and

- Establishing a level of security due diligence across the federal government.

In FY2010, the SMA group completed or updated the following key publications:

- Major revision of NIST SP 800-37, *Guide for Applying the Risk*

Management Framework to Federal Information Systems: A Security Life Cycle Approach, working in cooperation with the Office of the Director of National Intelligence (ODNI), the Department of Defense (DOD), and the Committee on National Security Systems (CNSS), to develop a common process to authorize federal information systems for operation; and

- Revision of NIST SP 800-53A, *Guide for Assessing the Security Controls in Federal Information Systems and Organizations, Building Effective Security Assessment Plans*, in partnership with the ODNI, DOD, and CNSS to update assessment procedures for the security control catalog in NIST SP 800-53, Revision 3, *Recommended Security Controls for Federal Information Systems and Organizations* .

In addition to the above publications, the division collaborated with the Manufacturing Engineering Laboratory at NIST in reviewing comments received and updating the draft guide to industrial control system security, NIST SP 800-82, *Guide to Industrial Control Systems (ICS) Security: Supervisory Control and Data Acquisition (SCADA) Systems, Distributed Control Systems (DCS), and Other Control System Configurations Such as Programmable Logic Controllers (PLC)*.

In FY2011, CSD plans to continue its collaboration with the ODNI, the DOD, and the CNSS, in expanding the series of NIST SPs for a unified information security framework for the federal government. Updates to the following draft publications will be completed in FY2011:

- SP 800-39, *Integrated Enterprise-Wide Risk Management: Organization, Mission, and Information System View*;

- SP 800-30, *Risk Management Guide for Information Technology Systems; and*

- SP 800-137, *Information Security Continuous Monitoring for Federal Information Systems and Organizations.*

In addition, a systems and security engineering guideline and application security guideline will be completed.

http://csrc.nist.gov/sec-cert
Contact:
Dr. Ron Ross
(301) 975-5390
ron.ross@nist.gov

Federal Information Security Management Act (FISMA) Implementation Project – Phase II

Phase II of the FISMA Implementation Project focuses on building common understanding and reference guides for organizations applying the NIST suite of publications that support the Risk Management Framework (RMF), and for public and private sector organizations that provide security assessments of information systems for federal agencies. Security assessments determine the extent to which the security controls are implemented correctly, operating as intended, and producing the desired outcome with respect to meeting the security requirements for the system. Managerial, operational, and technical security controls, including information technology products and services used in security control implementation, are all included in security assessments.

Phase II includes the following five initiatives:

(i) **Training:** development of training courses, publication of Quick Start Guides (QSGs), and development of Frequently Asked Questions (FAQs) for establishing common under standing of the NIST standards and guidelines supporting the NIST RMF;

(ii) **Support Tools:** defining criteria for common reference programs, materials, checklists, technical guides, automated tools and techniques supporting implementation and assessment of SP 800-53-based security controls;

(iii) **Product and Services Assurance:** defining minimum criteria and guidelines for security assurances (to include test results from Security Content Automation Protocol [SCAP] tools and configuration checklists, etc. where applicable) in products and services supporting implementation and assessment of SP 800-53-based security controls in information system operational environments;

(iv) **International Organization for Standardization (ISO) Harmonization:** identifying common relationships and mappings of FISMA standards, guidelines, and requirements with:

    (i) the International Organization for Standardization/International Electrotechnical Commission (ISO/IEC) 27000 series information security management standards; and

    (ii) ISO/IEC 9000 and 17000 series quality management, and laboratory testing/inspection standards respectively. This harmonization is important for minimizing duplication of effort for orga-nizations that must demonstrate compliance to both FISMA and ISO require ments; and

(v) **Organizational Security Assessment Capability:** defining minimum capability and proficiency criteria for public and private sector organizations providing security assessment services for federal agencies drawing upon material from the above initiatives.

In FY2010, CSD completed the following activities:
- Developed initial drafts of a web-based and classroom-based training courses on the RMF, Applying the RMF to Federal In formation Systems;

- Completed draft QSGs and FAQs supporting the Select step of the 6-step NIST RMF (adding to the currently available QSGs and FAQs for the Categorize and Monitor steps);

- Made available two databases for users wishing to access the security controls provided in Appendix F and G of SP 800-53, Revision 3 (with errata corrections as of May 2010). They are:

1. A standalone SP 800-53 Revision 3 Reference Database Application that can be downloaded and installed on the user's computer system and that allows the user to search and display the SP 800-53 security control catalog in a variety of views, and to extract security controls in a variety of file formats;

2. A web database, containing the catalog of security controls from SP 800-53 Revision 3 that enables users to interactively search and display security control content on-line in a variety of views. This on-line database has been developed to help customers quickly and efficiently (a) browse the security controls, control enhancements, and supplemental guidance, including summarizing the controls by control class, control family and system impact baseline; and (b) search the security control catalog using user-specified keywords. Future revisions of the SP 800-53 security control catalog will be maintained in the on-line SP 800-53 database. Also, additional capability is planned for the on-line database, such as supporting the export of security control text into other popular data formats, and adding to the database assessment procedures from Appendix F of SP 800-53A for the SP 800-53 security controls.

- Conducted research and held meetings with security product and security service suppliers seeking their views on readily available artifacts and evidence that could provide assurances that SP 500-53 based security control products and services meet requirements in organization specific information system operational environments.

In FY2011, CSD intends to: develop QSGs and FAQs for the Implement, Assess and Authorize steps of the 6-step RMF; continue to extend the capability of the on-line SP 800-53 security control database by adding to the database relevant assessment procedures from SP 800-53A; update the current exemplary assessment cases for consistency with the assessment procedures in SP 800-53A; and, collaborate with standards bodies for developing additional mappings of NIST standards and guidelines supporting the RMF to international frameworks.

---

http://csrc.nist.gov/sec-cert
Contacts:
Mr. Arnold Johnson   Ms. Pat Toth
(301) 975-3247   (301) 975-5140
arnold.johnson@nist.gov   patricia.toth@nist.gov

Computer Security Resource Center (CSRC)

The Computer Security Resource Center (CSRC) is CSD's website and is one of the most visited websites at NIST. CSRC encourages broad sharing of information security tools and practices, provides a resource for information security standards and guidelines, and identifies and links key security web resources to support industry and government users. CSRC is an integral component of all of the work that we conduct and produce. It is our repository for anyone, public or private sector, wanting to access our documents and other valuable information security-related information. During FY2010, our division's two websites, CSRC and the National Vulnerability Database (NVD) had more than 214.8 million requests combined[1]. CSRC received a little over 49.1 million total requests. The NVD website within CSRC received over 165.7 million total requests.

TOTAL NUMBER OF WEBSITE REQUESTS: CSRC & NVD

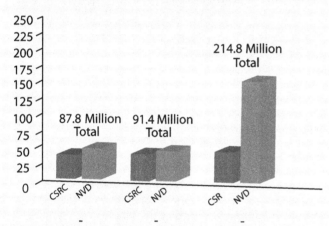

TOTAL NUMBER OF WEBSITE REQUESTS: CSRC & NVD

CSRC is the primary gateway for gaining access to NIST computer security publications, standards and guidelines, and serves as a vital link to our internal and external customers. The following documents can be found on CSRC: Drafts for public comment, Federal Information Processing Standards (FIPS), Special Publications (SPs), NIST Interagency Reports (NISTIRs), and ITL Security Bulletins.

The URL for the Publications homepage is: http://csrc.nist.gov/publications. Publications are organized by Topics, Family categories, and Legal Requirements to help users locate relevant information quickly.

During FY2010, the ten most popular downloaded documents from CSRC were:

1. SP 800-53 Revision 2, *Recommended Security Controls for Federal Information Systems,* and Revision 3, *Recommended Security Controls for Federal Information Systems and Organi-*

zations;

2. SP 800-30, *Risk Management Guide for Information Technology Systems;*

3. SP 800-53A, *Guide for Assessing the Security Controls in Federal Information Systems,* and 800-53A Revision 1, *Guide for Assessing the Security Controls in Federal Information Systems and Organizations, Building Effective Security Assessment Plans;*

4. SP 800-77, *Guide to IPsec VPNs;*

5. SP 800-115, *Technical Guide to Information Security Testing and Assessment;*

6. SP 800-34, *Contingency Planning Guide for Federal Information Systems;*

7. SP 800-94, *Guide to Intrusion Detection and Prevention Systems (IDPS);*

8. FIPS 140-2, *Security Requirements for Cryptographic Modules;*

9. SP 800-100, *Information Security Handbook: A Guide for Managers; and*

10. NISTIR 7628, *Guidelines for Smart Grid Cyber Security.*

CSRC is continuously updated with new information on various project pages. Some of the major highlights of CSRC during FY2010 were:

- Creation of a section for a new program titled the National Initiative for Cybersecurity Education (NICE) URL: http://www.nist.gov/nice/;

- Creation and updates of new validated products and certificate web pages for the Cryptographic Module Validation Program (CMVP) and Cryptographic Algorithm Validation Program (CAVP);

- Updates on the Small Business Community website with new information about workshops that took place in FY2010;

- Webcasts for the ISPAB quarterly meetings; and

- An on-line FISMA course titled *"Applying the Risk Management Framework to Federal Information Systems: A Security Life Cycle Approach."*

[1] These statistics are based from October 1, 2009 to September 30, 2010 timeframe. The total requests consist of webpages and file downloads.

In addition to CSRC, CSD maintains a publication announcement mailing list. This is a free e-mail list that notifies subscribers about publications that have been posted to the CSRC website. This e-mail list is a valuable tool for more than 10,000 subscribers including federal government employees, the private sector, educational institutions, and individuals with a personal interest in information technology (IT) security. Subscribers are notified when the CSD releases a publication, posts an announcement on CSRC, or when the CSD is hosting a security event. Individuals who are interested in learning more about this list or subscribing to it should visit this web page on CSRC for more information: http://csrc.nist.gov/publications/subscribe.html

Questions on the website should be sent to the CSRC Webmaster at: webmaster-csrc@nist.gov.

---

http://csrc.nist.gov/
Contact:
Mr. Patrick O'Reilly
patrick.oreilly@nist.gov

Federal Computer Security Program Managers' Forum

The Federal Computer Security Program Managers' Forum is an informal group that is sponsored by NIST to promote the sharing of security-related information among federal agencies. The Forum, which serves more than 1,030 members, strives to provide an ongoing opportunity for managers of federal information security programs to exchange information security materials in a timely manner, build upon the experiences of other programs, and reduce possible duplication of effort. It provides a mechanism for NIST to share information directly with federal agency information security program managers in fulfillment of NIST's leadership mandate under FISMA. It also assists NIST in establishing and maintaining relationships with other individuals or organizations that are actively addressing information security issues within the federal government. . NIST serves as the Secretariat of the Forum, providing necessary administrative and logistical support. Participation in Forum meetings is open to federal government employees who participate in the management of their organization's information security program. There are no membership dues.

The Forum hosts the Federal Agency Security Practices (FASP) website, maintains an extensive e-mail list, and holds bimonthly meetings and an annual two-day conference to discuss current issues and developments of interest to those responsible for protecting sensitive (unclassified) federal systems. The Forum plays a valuable role in helping NIST and other federal agencies develop and maintain a strong, proactive stance in the identification and resolution of new strategic and tactical IT security issues as they emerge.

Topics of discussion at Forum meetings in FY2010 included briefings from various federal agencies on Guidelines for Secure Use of Social Media by Federal Departments and Agencies; Supply Chain Risk Management Practices for Federal Information Systems; Trusted Internet Connections (TIC) Initiative Update; Maturing the Risk Management Framework through Government Cyber Partnership; Transitioning of Cryptographic Algorithms and Key Sizes, and a briefing and demonstration of the Department of State's risk scoring initiative.

This year's annual two-day conference featured updates on the computer security activities of the Government Accountability Office, NIST, the Office of Management and Budget, General Services Administration, and the Department of Homeland Security. Technical briefings included internet security threats, the National Vulnerability Database, cloud computing, identity management, draft NIST SP 800-39, *Integrated Enterprise-Wide Risk Management: Organization, Mission, and Information System View*, and *SP 800-30, Risk Management Guide for Information Technology*, and training initiatives.

The number of members on the e-mail list has grown steadily and provides a valuable resource for federal security program managers.

---

http://csrc.nist.gov/groups/SMA/forum/
Contact:
Mr. Kevin Stine
(301) 975-4483
kevin.stine@nist.gov
sec-forum@nist.gov

Federal Information Systems Security Educators' Association (FISSEA)

The Federal Information Systems Security Educators' Association (FISSEA), founded in 1987, is an organization run by and for information systems security professionals to assist federal agencies in meeting their information systems security awareness, training, and education responsibilities. FISSEA strives to elevate the general level of information systems security knowledge for the federal government and the federal workforce. FISSEA serves as a professional forum for the exchange of information and improvement of information systems security awareness, training, and education programs. It also seeks to assist the professional development of its members.

Federal Information Systems Security Educators' Association
AWARENESS • TRAINING • EDUCATION

FISSEA membership is open to information systems security professionals, professional trainers and educators, and managers responsible for information systems security training programs in federal agencies, as well as contractors of these agencies and faculty members of accredited educational institutions who are involved in information security training and education. There are no membership fees to join FISSEA; all that is required is a willingness to share products, information, and experiences. Business is administered by a 13-member executive board that meets monthly. Board members are elected to serve two-year terms.

Each year an award is presented to a candidate selected as FISSEA Educator of the Year; this award honors distinguished accomplishments in information systems security training programs. Brenda Oldfield of the Department of Homeland Security was awarded the Educator of the Year for 2009 at the 2010 FISSEA Conference.

The annual FISSEA Security Awareness, Training and Education Contest includes five categories from one of FISSEA's three key areas of Awareness, Training, and Education. The categories include, (1) awareness poster, (2) motivational item (aka: trinkets - pens, stress relief items, T-shirts. etc.), (3) awareness website, (4) awareness newsletter, and (5) role-based training and education. Winning entries for the security awareness contest are posted to the FISSEA website. The winners for the FY2010 contest were:

- Kathy Tucker of the Internal Revenue Service (IRS) Security Awareness Team for the motivational item;

- Ahmed Hussein of the Federal Aviation Administration (FAA) for the security newsletter;

- David Kurtz of the Bureau of the Public Debt for the awareness poster entry;

- Jim Henderson, U.S. Government Insider Threat Defense Center for the best security website; and

- Ruth Petersen, of the National Aeronautics and Space Administration (NASA) IT Security Awareness and Training Center, for the role-based training exercise.

FISSEA maintains a website, a list serve, and participates in a social networking site as a means of improving communication for its members. NIST assists FISSEA with its operations by providing staff support for several of its activities and by being FISSEA's host agency.

FISSEA membership in 2010 spanned federal agencies, industry, military, contractors, state governments, academia, the press, and foreign organizations to reach over 1,295 members in a total of ten countries. The 700 federal agency members represent 89 agencies from the executive and legislative branches of government.

On December 2, 2009, the twelfth free FISSEA workshop entitled, "Role-based Training Line of Business: Making it Work for You," was held and had over 70 participants (both in person and remotely via webinar) discussing what is currently available in role-based security training and what is needed. The workshop focused on the government-established Information Systems Security Line of Business Tier Two Training that encourages agencies to share information assurance, cyber security, and information system security role-based training best practices with each other. Presentations were given by participants from the Shared Service Providers, Department of Defense, Department of Veterans Affairs, NASA, and the Department of State.

The 2010 FISSEA conference was held at the National Institutes of Health (NIH) on March 23-25, 2010. Approximately 170 information systems security professionals and trainers attended, primarily from federal agencies, but including college and university faculty and staff, and representatives from firms that support federal information systems and security programs. This year's theme, "Unraveling the Enigma of Role-based Training", was chosen because effective role-based training continues to be a major challenge for federal agencies. While the goal is to have a staff that is adequately prepared to protect information assets within the constantly shifting cyber threat frontier, the path to that goal is not straightforward. Attendees had an opportunity to visit 24 vendors on the second day of the conference. FISSEA conferences continue to be a valuable forum in which federal information security professionals can learn of ongoing and planned training and education programs and initiatives. It also provides NIST the opportunity to provide assistance to departments and agencies as they work to meet their FISMA responsibilities.

The 2011 conference will return to NIST on March 15-17, 2011 and the theme is "Bridging to the Future – Emerging Trends in Cybersecurity". The theme was chosen to solicit presentations that reflect current projects, trends, and initiatives that will provide pathways to future solutions.

Stay aware, trained, and educated with FISSEA.

http://csrc.nist.gov/fissea
fisseamembership@nist.gov
Contacts:
Ms. Patricia Toth   Ms. Peggy Himes
(301) 975-5140   (301) 975-2489
patricia.toth@nist.gov   peggy.himes@nist.gov

Information Security Privacy Advisory Board (ISPAB)

The Information Security and Privacy Advisory Board (ISPAB) is a federal advisory committee that brings together senior professionals from industry, government, and academia to help advise NIST, the Office of Management and Budget (OMB), the Secretary of Commerce, and appropriate committees of the U.S. Congress about information security and privacy issues pertaining to unclassified federal government information systems.

The current ISPAB Board Members are Daniel Chenok (Chair), Jaren Doherty, Brian Gouker, Joseph Guirreri, Lynn McNulty, Alexander Popowycz, Lisa Schlosser, Fred B. Schneider, Ari Schwartz, Gale Stone, Matthew Thomlinson, and Peter Weinberger

The membership of the Board consists of eleven individuals and a Chairperson. The Director of NIST approves membership appointments and appoints the Chairperson. Each Board member serves for a four-year term. The Board's membership draws from experience at all levels of information security and privacy work. The members' careers cover government, industry, and academia. Members have worked in the Executive and Legislative branches of the federal government, civil service, senior executive service, the military, some of the largest corporations worldwide, small and medium-size businesses, and some of the top universities in the nation. The members' experience, likewise, covers a broad spectrum of activities including many different engineering disciplines, computer programming, systems analysis, mathematics, management, information technology auditing, and law. Members also have an extensive history of professional publications, and professional journalism. Members have worked (and in many cases, continue to work) on the development and evolution of some of the most important pieces of information security and privacy legislation in the federal government, including the Privacy Act of 1974, the Computer Security Act of 1987, the E-Government Act (including FISMA), and other e-government services and initiatives.

This advisory board of experienced, dynamic, and knowledgeable professionals provides NIST and the federal government with a rich, varied pool of people conversant with an extraordinary range of topics. They bring great depth to a field that has an exceptional rate of change. In FY2009 the board lost two long time members, Howard Schmidt and Rebecca Leng. They gained two more members, Gale Stone and Matthew Thomlinson.

The ISPAB was originally created by the Computer Security Act of 1987 (P.L. 100-35) as the Computer System Security and Privacy Advisory Board, and amended by Public Law 107-347, The E-Government Act of 2002, Title III, The Federal Information Security Management Act (FISMA) of 2002. As a result of FISMA, the Board's name was changed and its mandate was amended. The scope and objectives of the Board are to—

- Identify emerging managerial, technical, administrative, and physical safeguard issues relative to information security and privacy;

- Advise NIST, the Secretary of Commerce, and the Director of OMB on information security and privacy issues pertaining

to federal government information systems, including thorough review of proposed standards and guidelines developed by NIST; and

- Annually report the Board's findings to the Secretary of Commerce, the Director of OMB, the Director of the National Security Agency, and the appropriate committees of the Congress.

The Board usually meets three times per year and all meetings are open to the public. NIST provides the Board with its Secretariat. The Board has received numerous briefings from federal and private sector representatives on a wide range of privacy and security topics in the past year. Areas of interest that the Board followed in FY2010 were:

- Cloud Computing;

- Cyber Security Legislation;

- Health IT;

  o Embedded Software; and

  o Security of technology embedded in other systems;

- Identification and Authentication; and

- Federal Initiatives such as:

  o Cyber Education;

  o Security Issues in Broadband Plan;

  o SCAP – Security Automation and Vulnerability Management;

  o Threat Vector Initiatives;

  o Federal Risk and Authorization Management Pilot program (FedRAMP);

  o National Protection and Programs;

  o NASA Continuous Monitoring Program;

  o SCAP – Security Automation and Vulnerability Management;

  o Security Issues in Broadband Plan;

  o National Protection and Programs Directorate;

  o Key Management and Key Transition; and

http://csrc.nist.gov/ispab/
Contact:
Ms. Annie Sokol
(301) 975-2006
annie.sokol@nist.gov

Security Practices and Policies

The Federal Agency Security Practices (FASP) effort was initiated as a result of the success of the federal Chief Information Officers (CIO) Council's Federal Best Security Practices (BSP) pilot effort to identify, evaluate, and disseminate best practices for critical infrastructure protection and security. NIST was asked to undertake the transition of this pilot effort to an operational program. The result of that effort was the development of the FASP website. The FASP site contains agency policies, procedures and practices; the CIO Council's pilot BSPs; and a Frequently Asked Questions (FAQ) section.

Agencies are encouraged to submit their information security practices for posting on the FASP site so they may be shared with others in categories common to the NIST Special Publications (SP) 800 series. Any information on, or samples of, position descriptions for security positions and statements of work for contracting security related activities are also encouraged. In the past year, the site was consistently updated, removing a number of out-dated practices and adding new ones.

We also invite public and private organizations to submit their information security practices to be considered for inclusion on the website. Policies and procedures may be submitted to us in any area of information security, such as accreditation, audit trails, authorization of processing, budget planning and justification, certification, contingency planning, data integrity, disaster planning, documentation, hardware and system maintenance, identification and authentication, incident handling and response, life cycle, network security, personnel security, physical and environmental protection, production input/output controls, security policy, program management, review of security controls, risk management, security awareness training and education (including specific training course and awareness materials), and security planning.

In FY2011, we will continue to expand the number of sample practices and policies made available. We are currently identifying robust sources for more samples to add to this growing repository. We plan to take advantage of the advances in communication technology and combine this outreach with other outreach efforts in order to reach more people in the federal agencies and the public.

http://fasp.nist.gov/
Contact:
Ms. Peggy Himes
(301) 975-2489

Small and Medium-Sized Business (SMB) Outreach

What do a business' invoices have in common with e-mail? If both are done on the same computer, the business owner may want to think more about computer security. Information – payroll records, proprietary information, client or employee data – is essential to a business's success. A computer failure or system breach could cost a business anything from its reputation to damages and recovery costs. The small business owner who recognizes the threat of computer crime and takes steps to deter inappropriate activities is less likely to become a victim.

The vulnerability of any one small business may not seem significant to many, other than the owner and employees of that business. However, over 20 million U.S. businesses, comprising more than 95 percent of all U.S. businesses, are small and medium-size businesses (SMBs) of 500 employees or less. Therefore, a vulnerability common to a large percentage of SMBs could pose a threat to the nation's information infrastructure and economic base. SMBs frequently cannot justify an extensive security program or a full-time expert. Nonetheless, they confront serious security challenges.

The difficulty for these businesses is to identify security mechanisms and training that are practical and cost-effective. Such businesses also need to become more educated in terms of security so that limited resources are well applied to meet the most relevant and serious threats. To address this need, NIST, the Small Business Administration (SBA), and the Federal Bureau of Investigation (FBI) are cosponsoring a series of training meetings on computer security for small businesses. The purpose of the meetings is to provide an overview of information security threats, vulnerabilities, and corresponding protective tools and techniques, with a special emphasis on providing useful information that small business personnel can apply directly.

In FY2010, nineteen SMB outreach workshops were provided in seventeen cities: San Diego, CA; Santa Ana, CA; Charlotte, NC; Dallas, TX; Oklahoma City, OK; Cedar Rapids, IA; New Orleans, LA; Baton Rouge, LA; Salt Lake City, UT; Baltimore, MD; Tallahassee, FL; Jackson, MS; Des Moines, IA; Chicago, IL; Austin, TX; San Antonio, TX; and El Paso, TX.

In addition to the workshops, NIST in July 2010 also published a small business information security guide, NISTIR 7621, *Small Business Information Security: The Fundamentals*. This short document contains common sense information security advice for small businesses. As an additional outreach tool, NIST has also produced a video providing an overview of the information from the workshops.

http://sbc.nist.gov
Contact:
Mr. Richard Kissel
(301) 975-5017
richard.kissel@nist.gov

Security and Health Information Technology

Health information technology (HIT) makes it possible for healthcare providers to better manage patient care through secure use and sharing of health information, leading to improvements in healthcare quality, reduced medical errors, increased efficiencies in care delivery and administration, and improved population health. Central to reaching these goals is the assurance of the confidentiality, integrity, and availability of health information. The CSD works actively with government, industry, academia, and others to provide security tools, technologies, and methodologies that provide for the security and privacy of health information. As part of that work, CSD participates with, and provides technical advice to, agencies, organizations, and standards committees and panels that are shaping the HIT arena, including the Department of Health and Human Services' (HHS), Office of the National Coordinator for Health IT (ONC), and Office for Civil Rights (OCR).

In FY2010, CSD issued NISTIR 7497, *Security Architecture Design Process for Health Information Exchanges (HIEs)*. The purpose of this publication is to provide a systematic approach to designing a technical security architecture for the exchange of health information that leverages common government and commercial practices and that applies these practices specifically to the HIE domain. It seeks to assist organizations in ensuring that data protection is adequately addressed throughout the system development life cycle, and that these data protection mechanisms are applied when the organization develops technologies that enable the exchange of health information.

To assist organizations in implementing security and privacy safeguards to protect health information, NIST partnered with HHS/OCR to host the third annual HIPAA Security Rule Conference, "Safeguarding Health Information: Building Assurance through HIPAA Security," in May 2010. The purpose of the conference was to discuss challenges, ideas, and techniques for implementing the requirements of the HIPAA Security Rule. Nearly 400 attendees from federal, state, and local governments, academia, HIPAA covered entities and business associates, industry groups, and vendors heard from, and interacted with, healthcare, security, and privacy experts on technologies and methodologies for implementing the requirements of the HIPAA Security Rule, and the provisions outlined in the HITECH Act. Sessions covered a variety of management and technical topics related to the protection of health informa-

tion, including OCR's enforcement of the HIPAA Security and Privacy rules; techniques for developing risk assessments and contingency planning; breach notification; the security of health devices; and security considerations for the use of new media and wireless technologies in healthcare environments.

In FY2011, NIST plans to use security automation specifications to develop toolkits and checklists that will assist stakeholders in implementing the HIPAA Security Rule standards and implementation specifications, and assessing those implementations in their operational environments. NIST will also continue to collaborate with stakeholders on the broad range of activities necessary to safeguard health information.

Contacts:
Mr. Matthew Scholl   Mr. Kevin Stine
(301) 975-2941   (301) 975-4483
mscholl@nist.gov   kevin.stine@nist.gov

National Initiative for Cybersecurity Education (NICE)

NICE represents the evolution of the Comprehensive National Cybersecurity Initiative (CNCI) work on cybersecurity education. The scope of the initiative has been expanded from a federal focus to a larger national focus. NIST has assumed the overall coordination role for the effort, and is currently identifying resources needed, reviewing all related previous activities, and developing a strategic framework and a tactical plan of operation to support that framework. This expansion and the new overall coordination role by NIST are in response to the President's priorities as expressed in Chapter II, Building Capacity for a Digital Nation, of the President's Cyberspace Policy Review.

CSD is leading NIST's efforts to unify and coordinate federal resources to enable the larger national effort to improve cybersecurity awareness, education, and training for the entire country. This effort is targeted to all U.S. citizens of all ages (pre-school to senior citizens), and all types of professions whether it be academia (pre-school, K-12, college/universities), federal/state/local government, business partners (small-medium to large size businesses/companies), and local community groups (Girl Scouts, 4H, and much more). NICE has been divided into four different tracks, which can also be found on the NICE website.

1. ***Track 1:*** National Cybersecurity Awareness which is led by the Department of Homeland Security (DHS). The goal of this track is a national public awareness effort to guide the nation to a higher level of Internet safety by challenging the American public to be more vigilant about practicing good "cyber hygiene." It will persuade Americans to see Internet safety as a shared responsibility—at home, in the workplace, and in our communities—and demonstrate that shared responsibility by bringing together a coalition of federal, state and local

government, as well as private sector partners;

2. **Track 2:** Formal Cybersecurity Education which is led by the Department of Education. The goal of this track is to support the development of education programs encompassing K-12, higher education, and vocational programs related to cybersecurity. The focus is on the science, technology, engineering, and math disciplines in order to help provide a pipe line of skilled workers for private sector and government;

3. **Track 3:** Federal Cybersecurity Workforce Structure which is led by Office of Personnel Management (OPM). The goal of this track is to define cybersecurity jobs in the federal government and skills and competencies required. They will also identify new strategies to ensure federal agencies attract, recruit, and retain skilled employees to accomplish cybersecurity missions; and

4. **Track 4:** Cybersecurity Workforce Training and Professional Development. This track is led by Department of Defense, Office of the Director of National Intelligence, and DHS. The goal of this track is to identify and manage the cybersecurity training and professional development required for federal government civilian, military, and contractor personnel..

During FY2010, the following major accomplishment and highlights were achieved:

- On June 29-30, 2010, the Cybersecurity Workforce Training and Professional Development Track hosted its second leadership conference at the Federal Law Enforcement Training Center (FLETC) in Glynco, Georgia;

- On July 14, 2010, The National Cybersecurity Awareness Track announced the winners of the National Cyber Challenge at the White House; the recipients shook hands with the Secretary of DHS and were presented with awards for their submissions;

- On August 11-12, 2010, the successful NICE Kick-off Workshop was held.

- On August 20, 2010, the NICE Leader participated in a panel discussion on cybersecurity workforce at U.S.-CERT Government Forum of Incident Response and Security Team (GFIRST) sixth Annual National Conference in San Antonio, TX;

- On August 23, 2010, the NICE Leader and Track 4 representatives participated in a planning session for a proposed Global Institute for Cybersecurity Research (GICSR) at the Center for Technology Innovation Exploration Park at the Kennedy Space Center, FL. along with the Florida Institute of Technology, Brevard Community College, NASA, Space Florida, and

others;

- On September 10, 2010, Track 2 (Formal Cybersecurity Education) held discussions with the National Cyber Security Alliance (NCSA) and CyberWatch regarding efforts to work with those organizations so they can serve as the nucleus for the education community at large to form an organization with which the U. S. Government can engage to address shared cybersecurity education goals and interests;

- On September 18, 2010, Track 3 (Federal Cybersecurity Work force Structure) in conjunction with the NICE, OPM launched the Cybersecurity Competency Model Survey;

- Input for the FY2012 budget build process was generated and sent forward;

- The CSD created the NICE website. The website development has completed phase I. Phase II will begin in FY2011; this effort will greatly improve the website and also provide more information to the public (URL: http://www.nist.gov/nice/); and

- The initiation of the NICE leadership plan development process, combined with various very positive print and radio in terviews as well as participation on a number of panels, comprise the accomplishments and highlights of NICE to date.

The NICE website went live in May 2010, and is hosted on the NIST CSD's CSRC. The first phase was to provide information on the beginning stages of the NICE efforts. The NICE website is a joint effort and receives contribution of material through multiple agencies. Phase II of the NICE website will feature an interactive experience, new pages, and updated information.

In FY2011, CSD will lead the tracks in: completing the staffing process for NICE as well as the strategic plan development process; conducting another national level workshop event as well as a presidential level event to highlight major accomplishments of NICE.

---

http://www.nist.gov/nice
Contact:
Dr. Ernest L. McDuffie, Ph.D.
(301) 975-8897
ernest.mcduffie@nist.gov

Smart Grid Cyber Security

Recognizing the benefit of focusing NIST's technical expertise on one of the nation's most pressing issues, Congress, in the Energy Independence and Security Act of 2007 (EISA), called on NIST to take a leadership role in ensuring an interoperable, secure, and open energy infrastructure that will enable all electric resources, including demand-side resources, to contribute to an efficient, reliable electricity network. Cyber security for the electricity grid is a critical issue due to the increasing potential of cyber attacks and incidents against this critical sector as it becomes more and more interconnected. Existing vulnerabilities might allow an attacker to penetrate a network, gain access to control software, and alter load conditions to destabilize the grid in unpredictable ways.

To help ensure that the cyber security requirements of the Smart Grid are addressed in the NIST Smart Grid Interoperability Framework, NIST established the Smart Grid Cyber Security Working Group (CSWG) which now has more than 500 volunteer members from the public and private sectors, academia, regulatory organizations, federal agencies, and representatives from five countries. The CSWG is led by CSD. This group and its work are open to the public.

To complete the work, there are ten working groups that focus on specific components of the cyber security strategy:

- Vulnerability analysis;

- Bottom-up security issues;

- Security architecture;

- High level requirements;

- Research and development;

- Cryptography and key management;

- Testing and certification;

- Security specifications for smart meters;

- Privacy; and

- Standards assessment.

Cyber security is being addressed in a complementary and integral process that has resulted in a comprehensive set of high level cyber security requirements. These requirements were developed using a risk assessment process that is defined in the draft NISTIR 7628, *Guidelines for Smart Grid Cyber Security*, which describes the CSWG's overall cyber security strategy for the Smart Grid. The document, issued for comment in August 2010, identifies security-relevant use cases, logical interface diagrams and interface categories, vulnerability classes abstracted from other relevant cyber security documents, specific issues applicable to the Smart Grid, privacy concerns, security requirements applicable to the Smart Grid, and a cross-reference matrix of applicable security require-

ments from various standards documents. An introductory synopsis is being developed for the three volume document.

Future work includes working with the subgroups of the Smart Grid Interoperability Panel in order to integrate cyber security into other work efforts. The Interoperability Panel is focusing on the standards needed to ensure interoperability of Smart Grid components and system. The CSWG will work to ensure that security is incorporated into standards where appropriate. The CSWG will also conduct a number of outreach meetings to discuss NISTIR 7628 with a wide range of audiences.

---

http://collaborate.nist.gov/twiki-sggrid/bin/view/SmartGrid/Cyber-SecurityCTG
Contact:
Ms. Marianne Swanson
(301) 975-3293
marianne.swanson@nist.gov

Supply Chain Risk Management

The ever broadening reliance upon globally sourced information system equipment exposes federal information systems and networks to an increasing risk of exploitation through counterfeit materials, malicious code, or untrustworthy products. NIST participation in the President's Comprehensive National Cybersecurity Initiative (CNCI) Initiative 11, Develop Multi-Pronged Approach for Global Supply Chain Risk Management, which is co-chaired by the Department of Defense (DoD) and Department of Homeland Security (DHS), will provide federal agencies with a standard and a toolkit of acquisition, technical, and intelligence resources to manage supply chain risk to a level commensurate with the criticality of information systems or networks. In 2010, NIST also issued a grant to the University of Maryland, RH Smith School of Business, Supply Chain Management Center to research the membership of leading associations to learn more about industry practices.

NIST, in coordination with DoD, DHS, and Department of State issued for public review in June 2010 draft NISTIR 7622, *Supply Chain Risk Management Practices for Federal Information Systems*. This document discusses the following topics:

- Determining which procurements should consider supply chain risk;

- Working with the procurement office, legal counsel, information system security personnel, and other appropriate agency stakeholders to help mitigate supply chain risk through the careful selection of security and supply chain contractual requirements;

- Resolving residual supply chain risk by implementing additional applicable practices contained in the document and augmenting the baseline of security controls defined for the information system; and

- Describing the key roles and responsibilities within the organization as they relate to supply chain risk management.

NIST intends to expand the NISTIR document into a NIST SP when the practices and organizational structure and methodologies have been piloted under the auspice of the CNCI Initiative.

Contact:
Mr. Jon Boyens
(301) 975-5549
jon.boyens@nist.gov

Cryptographic Validation Programs and Laboratory Accreditation

The Cryptographic Algorithm Validation Program (CAVP) and the Cryptographic Module Validation Program (CMVP) were developed by NIST to support the needs of the user community for strong, independently tested and commercially available cryptographic algorithms and modules. Through these programs, NIST works with the commercial sector and the cryptographic community to achieve security, interoperability, and assurance of correct implementation. The goal of these programs is to promote the use of validated algorithms, modules and products and to provide federal agencies with a security metric to use in procuring cryptographic modules. The testing performed by accredited laboratories and the validation performed by these two programs provides this metric. Federal agencies, industry, and the public can choose cryptographic modules and/or products containing cryptographic modules from the CMVP Validated Modules List and have confidence in the claimed level of security and assurance of correct implementation.

Cryptographic algorithm and cryptographic module testing and validation are based on underlying published standards and guidance that is developed within the CSD in collaboration with many other organizations. As federal agencies are required to use validated cryptographic modules for the protection of sensitive non-classified information, the validated modules and the validated algorithms they contain represent the culmination and delivery of the division's cryptography based work to the end user.

The CAVP and the CMVP are separate, collaborative programs based on a partnership between NIST's CSD and the Communication Security Establishment Canada (CSEC). The programs provide federal agencies—in the United States and Canada—confidence that a validated cryptographic algorithm has been implemented correctly and that a validated cryptographic module meets a claimed level of security assurance. The CAVP and the CMVP validate algorithms and modules used in a wide variety of products, including secure Internet browsers, secure radios, smart cards, space-based communications, munitions, security tokens, storage devices, and products supporting Public Key Infrastructure and electronic commerce. A module may be a standalone product such as a virtual private network (VPN), smartcard or toolkit or one module may be used in several products, so a small number of modules may be incorporated within hundreds of products. Likewise, the CAVP validates cryptographic algorithms that may be integrated in one or more cryptographic modules.

The two validation programs (the CAVP and CMVP) provide documented methodologies for conformance testing through defined sets of security requirements. For the CAVP, these are found in the individual validation system documents containing the validation test suites required to assure the algorithm has been implemented correctly The validation system documents are designed for each FIPS-Approved and NIST-Recommended cryptographic algorithm. For the CMVP, these security requirements are found in FIPS 140-2, *Security Requirements for Cryptographic Modules*, and the associated test metrics and methods in Derived Test Requirements for FIPS 140-2, *Security Requirements for Cryptographic Modules*. The FIPS 140-2 Annexes reference the underlying cryptographic algorithm standards or methods. Federal agencies are required to use modules that were validated as conforming to the provisions of FIPS 140-2. *The CMVP developed Derived Test Requirements associated with FIPS 140-2 to define the security requirements and test metrics and methods to ensure repeatability of tests and equivalency in results across the testing laboratories.*

The CMVP reviews the cryptographic modules validations and, as a byproduct of the review, is introduced to emerging and/or changing technologies and the evolution of operating environments and complex systems during the module validation review activities. Likewise, the CAVP reviews the cryp

General Flow of FIPS 140-2 Testing and Validation

tographic algorithm validation requests submitted by the accredited laboratories. With these insights, the CAVP and CMVP can perform research and development of new test metrics and methods as they evolve. Based on this research, the CAVP and CMVP publish implementation guidance to assist vendors, testing laboratories and the user community in the latest programmatic and technical guidance. This guidance provides clarity, consistency of interpretation and insight for successful conformance testing, validation and revalidation.

The unique position of the validation programs gives them the opportunity to acquire insight during the validation review activities results in practical, timely and up to date guidance needed by the testing laboratories and vendors to move their modules and products out to the user community in a timely and cost effective manner but with the assurance of third-party conformance testing. This also provides a repository of knowledge and insight to leverage for future standards development.

The CAVP and the CMVP have stimulated improved quality and security assurance of cryptographic modules. The latest set of statistics which are collected quarterly from each of the testing laboratories show that eight percent of the cryptographic algorithms and 61 percent of the cryptographic modules brought in for voluntary testing had security flaws that were corrected during testing. Without this program, the federal government would have had less than a 50 percent chance of buying correctly implemented cryptography. To date, over 1,440 cryptographic module validation certificates have been issued, representing over 3,100 modules that were validated by the CMVP. These modules have been developed by more than 335 domestic and international vendors.

The CAVP issued 1,475 algorithm validations and the CMVP issued 221 module validation certificates in FY2010. The number of algorithms and modules submitted for validation continues to grow, representing significant growth in the number of validated products expected to be available in the future.

---

http://csrc.nist.gov/groups/STM

Contacts: CMVP Contact: CAVP Contact:
Mr. Randall J. Easter   Ms. Sharon Keller
(301) 975-4641   (301) 975-2910
randall.easter@nist.gov   sharon.keller@nist.gov

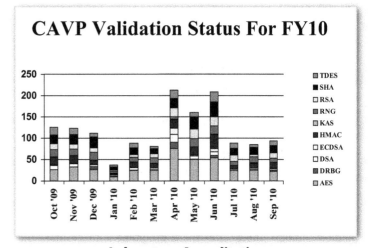

Laboratory Accreditation

The commercial Cryptographic and Security Testing (CST) laboratories accredited by the National Voluntary Laboratory Accreditation Program (NVLAP) provide vendors of cryptographic modules

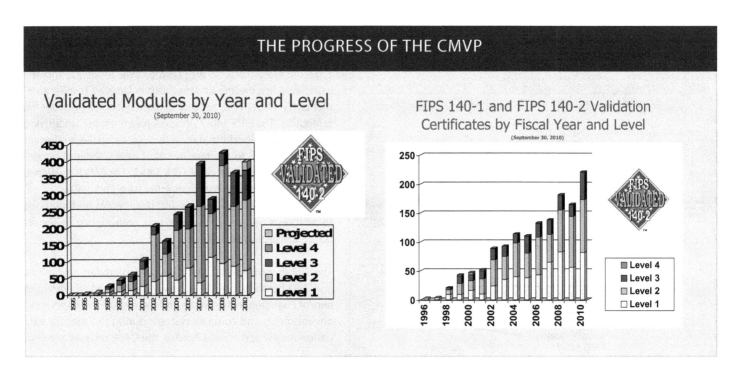

a choice of testing facilities and promote healthy competition. Vendors of cryptographic modules and algorithms use independent, private sector testing laboratories accredited as CST laboratories by NVLAP to have their cryptographic modules validated by the CMVP and their cryptographic algorithms validated by the-CAVP. The CMVP collaborates with NVLAP by providing the technical assessors for the laboratory audits and accreditation activities. As the worldwide growth and use of cryptographic modules have increased, demand to meet the testing needs for both algorithms and modules developed by vendors has also grown. There are currently 19 accredited laboratories in the U. S., Canada, Germany, Spain, Japan, Taiwan R.O.C., and Australia. NVLAP has received several applications for the accreditation of CST Laboratories,both domestically and internationally. A complete list of accredited laboratories may be found at http://csrc.nist.gov/groups/STM/testing_labs/.

NVLAP: http://www.nist.gov/pml/nvlap/
CMVP and CAVP: http://csrc.nist.gov/groups/STM/CMVP
Contact:

CMVP Contact:	CAVP Contact:
Mr. Randall J. Easter	Ms. Sharon Keller
(301) 975-4641	(301) 975-2910
randall.easter@nist.gov	sharon.keller@nist.gov

Automated Security Testing and Test Suite Development

Federal Information Processing Standards (FIPS) and NIST Special Publications (SP) define the FIPS-recommended and NIST-approved cryptographic algorithms recognized by the federal government. The detailed specifications of the cryptographic algorithms and how they are to be implemented is contained within these documents. Automated security testing of these cryptographic algorithms provides a uniform way to assure that the cryptographic algorithm implementation adheres to the detailed specifications. Validation test suites are designed and developed by the CAVP. These tests exercise the mathematical formulas detailed in the algorithm to assure the detailed specifications are implemented correctly and completely. If the implementer deviates from these instructions or excludes any part of the instructions, the validation test will fail, indicating that the algorithm implementation does not function properly or is incomplete.

There are several types of validation tests, all designed to satisfy the testing requirements of the cryptographic algorithms and their specifications. These include, but are not limited to, Known Answer Tests, Monte Carlo Tests, and Multi-Block Message Tests. The Known Answer Tests are designed to test the conformance of the implementation under test (IUT) to the various specifications in the reference. This involves testing the components of the algorithm to assure that they are implemented correctly. The Monte Carlo Test is designed to exercise the entire IUT. This test is designed to detect the presence of implementation flaws that

are not detected with the controlled input of the Known Answer Tests. The types of implementation flaws detected by this validation test include pointer problems, insufficient allocation of space, improper error handling, and incorrect behavior of the IUT. The Multi-Block Message Test (MMT) is designed to test the ability of the implementation to process multi-block messages, which require the chaining of information from one block to the next.

Automated security testing and test suite development are integral components of the CAVP. The CAVP encompasses validation testing for FIPS-approved and NIST-recommended cryptographic algorithms. Cryptographic algorithm validation is a prerequisite to the CMVP. The testing of cryptographic algorithm implementations is performed by third-party laboratories that are accredited as Cryptographic and Security Testing (CST) laboratories by the National Voluntary Laboratory Accreditation Program (NVLAP). The CAVP develops and maintains a Cryptographic Algorithm Validation System (CAVS) tool that automates the cryptographic algorithm validation testing. The CAVS currently has algorithm validation testing for the following cryptographic algorithms:

THE PROGRESS OF THE CAVP

CAVP Validation Status By FYs

CAVP Validated Implementation Actual Numbers

Updated As Thursday, November 04, 2010

FiscalYear	AES	DES	DSA	DRBG	ECDSA	HMAC	KAS	RNG	RSA	SHA	SJ	TDES	Total
FY1996	0	2	0	0	0	0	0	0	0	0	0	0	2
FY1997	0	11	6	0	0	0	0	0	0	7	2	0	26
FY1998	0	27	9	0	0	0	0	0	0	6	0	0	42
FY1999	0	30	14	0	0	0	0	0	0	12	1	0	57
FY2000	0	29	7	0	0	0	0	0	0	12	1	28	77
FY2001	0	41	15	0	0	0	0	0	0	28	0	51	135
FY2002	30	44	21	0	0	0	0	0	0	59	6	58	218
FY2003	66	49	24	0	0	0	0	0	0	63	3	73	278
FY2004	82	41	17	0	0	0	0	28	22	77	0	70	337
FY2005	145	54	31	0	14	115	0	108	80	122	2	102	773
FY2006	131	3	33	0	19	87	0	91	63	120	1	83	631
FY2007	239	0	63	0	35	127	0	137	130	171	1	136	1039
FY2008	271	0	77	4	41	158	0	137	129	191	0	122	1130
FY2009	374	0	71	23	33	193	3	142	143	224	1	138	1345
FY2010	399	0	71	32	40	180	6	150	156	240	0	143	1417
Total	1737	331	459	59	182	860	9	793	723	1332	18	1004	7507

In FY2011, the CAVP expects to augment the CAVS tool to provide algorithm validation testing for:

- RSA2 (as specified in FIPS 186-3, *Digital Signature Standard (DSS)*, dated June 2009);

- SP 800-108, *Recommendation for Key Derivation Using Pseudorandom Functions*, dated November 2008;

- SP 800-106, *Randomized Hashing for Digital Signatures*, dated February 2009; and

- SP 800-56B, *Recommendation for Pair-Wise Key Establishment Schemes Using Integer Factorization Cryptography*, dated August 2009.

Crytographic Algorithm	Special Publications or FIPS
Triple Data Encrytion Standard (TDES)	SP 800-67, *Recommendation for the Triple Data Encryption Algorithm (TDEA) Block Cipher*, and SP 800-38A, *Recommendation for Block Cipher Modes of Operation – Methods and Techniques*
Advanced Encryption Standard (AES)	FIPS 197, *Advanced Encryption Standard, and SP 800-38A*
Digital Signature Standard (DSS)	FIPS 186-2, *Digital Signature Standard (DSS,) with change notice 1, dated October 5, 2001*
Digital Signature Standard (DSS)	FIPS 186-3, *Digital Signature Standard (DSS), dated June 2009*
Elliptic Curve Digital Signature Algorithm (ECDSA)	FIPS 186-2, *Digital Signature Standard (DSS,) with change notice 1, dated October 5, 2001* and ANSI X9.62
Elliptic Curve Digital Signature Algorithm (ECDSA)	FIPS 186-3, *Digital Signature Standard (DSS), dated June 2009* and ANSI X9.62
RSA algorithm	ANSI X9.31 and *Public Key Cryptography Standards (PKCS) #1 v2.1: RSA Cryptography Standard-2002*
Hashing algorithms SHA-1, SHA-224, SHA-256, SHA-384, and SHA-512	FIPS 180-3, *Secure Hash Standard (SHS), dated October 2008*
Random number generator (RNG) algorithms	FIPS 186-2 Appendix 3.1 and 3.2; ANSI X9.62 Appendix A.4
Deterministic Random Bit Generators (DRBG)	SP 800-90, *Recommendation for Random Number Generation Using Deterministic Random Bit Generators*
Keyed-Hash Message Authentication Code (HMAC	FIPS 198, *The Keyed-Hash Message Authentication Code (HMAC)*
Counter with Cipher Block Chaining-Message Authentication Code (CCM) mode	SP 800-38C, *Recommendation for Block Cipher Modes of Operation: the CCM Mode for Authentication and Confidentiality*
Cipher-based Message Authentication Code (CMAC) Mode for Authentication	SP 800-38B, *Recommendation for Block Cipher Modes of Operation: The CMAC Mode for Authentication*
Galois/Counter Mode (GCM) GMAC Mode of Operation	SP 800-38D, *Recommendation for Block Cipher Modes of Operation: Galois/Counter Mode (GCM) and GMAC*, dated November 2007
XTS Mode of Operation	SP800-38E, *Recommendation for Block Cipher Modes of Operation: The XTS-AES Mode for Confidentiality on Block-Oriented Storage Devices, dated January 2010*
Key Agreement Schemes and Key Confirmation	SP 800-56A, *Recommendation for Pair-Wise Key Establishment Schemes Using Discrete Logarithm Cryptography, dated March 2007*

http://csrc.nist.gov/groups/STM/cavp
Contact:
Ms. Sharon Keller
(301) 975-2910
sharon.keller@nist.gov

ISO Standardization of Security Requirements for Cryptographic Modules

CSD has contributed to the activities of the International Organization for Standardization/International Electrotechnical Commission (ISO/IEC), which issued ISO/IEC 19790, Security Requirements for Cryptographic Modules, on March 1, 2006, and ISO/IEC 24759, Test Requirements for Cryptographic Modules, on July 1, 2008. These efforts bring consistent testing of cryptographic modules to the global community.

ISO/IEC JTC 1/SC 27 has progressed on the revision of ISO/IEC 19790 of which Randall J. Easter of CSD is an editor. In January 2010, the first working draft was circulated for national body comment. This first working draft included many of the proposed changes identified from the NIST working group revision of FIPS 140-2. The second working draft was circulated for national body comment during August 2010. The second working draft incorporated accepted national body comments received from the first working draft and additional feedback from the NIST working group revision of FIPS 140-2. The third working draft is currently in revision with delivery for national body comment during January 2011.

http://csrc.nist.gov/groups/STM/cmvp/index.html
Contact:
Mr. Randall J. Easter
(301) 975-4641
randall.easter@nist.gov

Security Management and Assurance (SMA) Group Guidelines and Documents

SMA's guidelines and documents along with the abstracts to these documents can be found in the Publications section on pages 51-60.

Cryptographic Technology Group

Develop and improve mechanisms to protect the integrity, confidentiality, and authenticity of federal agency information by developing security mechanisms, standards, testing methods, and supporting infrastructure requirements and procedures.

Overview

The Cryptographic Technology Group's work in cryptographic mechanisms addresses topics such as hash algorithms, symmetric and asymmetric cryptographic techniques, key management and authentication. In cryptographic protocols, focus areas include Internet security services, security applications, identity management, and smart tokens. The Group continued to make an impact in the field of cryptography both within and outside the federal government by collaborating with national and international agencies, academic and research organizations, and standards bodies to develop interoperable security standards and guidelines.

Federal agency collaborators include the National Security Agency (NSA), the National Telecommunications and Information Administration (NTIA), the Election Assistance Commission (EAC), and the Federal Voting Assistance Program (FVAP). International agencies include the Communications Security Establishment of Canada, and Australia's Defense Signals Agency and Centrelink. National and international standards bodies include the American Standards Committee (ASC) X9 (financial industry standards), the International Organization for Standardization (ISO), the Institute of Electrical and Electronics Engineers (IEEE), the Internet Engineering Task Force (IETF), and the Trusted Computing Group (TCG). Industry collaborators include the Internet Corporation for Assigned Names and Numbers (ICANN), VeriSign, Certicom, Entrust Technologies, Microsoft, Orion Security, RSA Security, Voltage Security, Juniper, and Cisco. Academic collaborators include Katholieke Universiteit Leuven, George Mason University, Danmarks Tekniske Universitet, George Washington University, SDU Odense, UC Davis, Malaga University, and Yale University. Academic and research organizations include the International Association for Cryptologic Research (IACR), the European Network of Excellence in Cryptology (ECRYPT) II, the Japanese Cryptography Research and Evaluation Committees (CRYPTREC) and the National Electrical Manufacturers Association (NEMA).

Strong cryptography, developed in part by the Group, can be used to improve the security of information systems and the information they process. Users can then take advantage of the availability of secure applications in the marketplace that is made possible by the appropriate use of standardized high quality cryptography. This work also supports the NIST's Personal Identity Verification (PIV) project in response to the Homeland Security Presidential Directive 12 (HSPD-12); for further details see Personal Identity Verification (PIV) section under the Systems and Emerging Technologies Security Research Group.

Cryptographic Standards Toolkit

Hash Algorithms and the *Secure Hash Standard* (SHA)-3 Competition

The Cryptographic Technology Group is responsible for the maintenance and development of the *Secure Hash Standard* in FIPS 180-3. A hash algorithm processes a message, which can be very large, and produces a condensed representation, called the message digest. A cryptographic hash algorithm is a fundamental component of many cryptographic functions, such as digital signature algorithms, key derivation functions, keyed-hash message authentication codes, or random number generators. Cryptographic hash algorithms are frequently used in Internet protocols or in other security applications.

In 2005, researchers developed an attack that threatens the security of the NIST-approved, government hash algorithm standard, SHA-1. Since 2005, researchers at NIST and elsewhere have also discovered several generic limitations in the basic Merkle-Damgard construct that is used in SHA-1 and most other existing hash algorithms. To address these vulnerabilities, NIST opened a public competition in November 2007 to develop a new cryptographic hash algorithm, which will be called "SHA-3", and will augment the hash algorithms currently specified in FIPS 180-3.

CSD selected 51 first round candidates from the 64 entries received by the submission deadline of October 31, 2008. The first round candidates selected were invited to present their algorithms at the First SHA-3 Candidate Conference in Leuven, Belgium in February 2009. Based on the reviews from the international cryptographic community, CSD selected 14 second round candidates on July 24, 2009, and asked them to submit adjusted algorithms for a second round of competition by September 15, 2009. The second round of the competition started in October 2009. Since then, the CSD and the cryptographic community have conducted cryptanalysis, implementation and performance reviews of the remaining candidates. Some of the research was funded by the American Recovery and Reinvestment Act.

CSD held the Second SHA-3 Candidate Conference at the University of California, Santa Barbara in August 2010 to evaluate the 14 remaining candidates. The conference was well-attended and substantial analysis results were presented. CSD plans to announce four to six finalists early in fiscal year 2011 and will allow another period of adjustment to the finalists' algorithms. One year of public review is allocated for the finalists, and a final SHA-3 Candidate Conference is planned for Spring 2012 where the results of community review and analysis will be presented on the revised algorithms. CSD intends to complete the competition and announce the SHA-3 winner in 2012.

Contact:
Ms. Shu-jen Chang
(301) 975-2940
shu-jen.chang@nist.gov

Block Cipher Modes of Operation

In January 2010, SP 800-38E, *Recommendation for Block Cipher Modes of Operation: the XTS-AES Mode for Confidentiality on Block-Oriented Storage Devices*, was published in which the XTS-AES mode by reference to the specification in IEEE Standard 1619-2007 was approved. The XTS-AES mode is designed to encrypt data for storage applications without expansion of the data in order to avoid disrupting existing data pathways. Although this design precludes the incorporation of a tag-based authentication method, XTS-AES is engineered to mitigate the resulting vulnerability for manipulation of the encrypted data.

A draft addendum to SP 800-38A, *Recommendation for Block Cipher Modes of Operation: Methods and Techniques*, was issued for public review with comments due in August 2010. It contained three variants of the Cipher Block Chaining (CBC) mode that employ the "ciphertext stealing" padding method. Plain CBC mode requires input messages whose length is a multiple of the block size; the variants extend this domain to messages of any length that is not strictly smaller than the block size. With conventional padding methods, the length of the ciphertext expands by the number of padding bits; the ciphertext stealing variants are designed to avoid such expansion. NIST published the final addendum in October 2010.

NIST received an additional new mode submission this year in the area of format-preserving encryption, as well as a substantial revision and supplement to one of the two previous submissions. A format might be a credit card number or a social security number, and a format preserving encryption mode enables the selective encryption of the formatted data, without affecting the surrounding data. NIST expects to initiate the approval process for one of the three submissions in this area during the coming year.

Contact:
Dr. Morris Dworkin
(301) 975-2354
morris.dworkin@nist.gov

Key Management

NIST continues to address the needs of the federal government by defining the basic principles required for key management, including key establishment, wireless applications, and the Public Key Infrastructure (PKI). The requirements for key management continue to expand as new types of devices and connectivity mechanisms become available (e.g., laptops and smart cell phones).

In December 2009, NIST published the final version of SP 800-57, *Recommendation for Key Management - Part 3: Application-Specific Key Management Guidance*. This document includes the protocol specific guidance for protocols such as Internet Protocol Security (IPsec), Transport Layer Security Secure/Multipurpose Internet Mail Extensions (S/MIME), Kerberos, Over-the-Air Rekeying and Domain Name System Security Extensions (DNSSEC). It also contains guidance on using PKI and Encrypted File Systems. It is anticipated that other sections will be added in the future to provide guidance in other specific applications and protocols (e.g., the Secure Shell protocol and Trusted Platform Modules).

In June 2010, NIST requested comments on a draft of SP 800-130, *A Framework for Designing Cryptographic Key Management Systems (CKMS)*. SP 800-130 identifies and discusses the components of a CKMS and provides requirements for CKMS design specifications conforming to the Framework. The publication is intended to encourage CKMS designers and others to consider the factors that make a comprehensive CKMS and thus improve CKMS security. A workshop was held in September 2010 to discuss both the Framework and comments received on the draft, and to discuss the development of a profile of the Framework for U.S. government CKMS. Information about the workshop is available at http://csrc.nist.gov/groups/ST/key_mgmt/.

There were several significant publications in the area of key derivation over the last year. SP 800-108, *Recommendation for Key Derivation Using Pseudorandom Functions*, was modified in October 2009 to provide further clarification on the input format for key derivation functions. This document, originally published in 2008, specifies techniques for the derivation of additional keying material from a secret key using pseudorandom functions. Draft SP 800-132, *Recommendation for Password-based Key Derivation Part 1: Storage Applications*, was posted for public comment in June 2010. This publication specifies techniques for the derivation of master keys from passwords to protect electronic data in storage environments. The final version of SP 800-132 will be available in early FY2011. SP 800-56C, *Recommendation for Key Derivation through Extraction-then-Expansion*, which specifies a general technique for the derivation of keying material from a shared secret value established by a key establishment scheme defined in NIST SP 800-56A, *Recommendation for Pair-Wise Key Establishment Schemes Using Discrete Logarithm Cryptography*, and SP 800-56B, *Recommendation for Pair-Wise Key Establishment Schemes Using Integer Factorization Cryptography*, was posted for public comment in September 2010.

Many key derivation functions used in widely-used protocols and applications do not conform to the ones approved in SP 800-56 A, B and C, or in SP 800-108. However, security analysis indicates that these non-conforming key derivative functions provide adequate security in the contexts of their own protocols. SP 800-135, *Recommendation for Existing Application-Specific Key Derivation Functions*, was developed to provide a methodology for approving these key derivative functions. A draft of this Recommendation was posted for public comment in August 2010 and should be finalized in early FY2011.

All of the above NIST Special Publications are available at:

http://csrc.nist.gov/publications/PubsSPs.html.
http://csrc.nist.gov/groups/ST/key_mgmt/

Contacts:
Ms. Elaine Barker   Mr. Quynh Dang
(301) 975-2911   (301) 975-3610
ebarker@nist.gov   qdang@nist.gov

Dr. Lily Chen   Dr. Meltem Sönmez Turan
(301) 975-6974   (301) 975-4391
llchen@nist.gov   meltem.turan@nist.gov

Transitioning of Cryptographic Algorithms and Key Lengths

At the start of the 21st century, NIST began the task of providing cryptographic key management guidance. An essential part of that guidance is planning ahead for changes in the use of cryptography because of algorithm breaks or the availability of more powerful computing techniques. To assist agencies and to recognize the speed at which the use of cryptography is changing, in 2010, NIST requested public comments on Draft SP 800-131, *Recommendation for the Transitioning of Cryptographic Algorithms and Key Sizes*. In addition to requesting public comments, the transition plan was presented at various forums and conferences in order to obtain a broader response.

SP 800-131 provides a detailed transition schedule for the use of the families of algorithms approved by NIST, such as the algorithms used for encryption, digital signatures, hash functions, random number generation, key establishment and several others. The guidance specifies when an algorithm or key size is foreseen to be safe to use, when it can be used as long as some level of risk is accepted, when it can be used for legacy applications, and when its use should be discontinued because projections indicate that the algorithm or key length will no longer provide adequate security. This transition plan will be finalized in early FY2011, and will have a significant impact on most federal users and vendors of cryptographic modules.

CryptoTransitions@nist.gov
Contacts:
Ms. Elaine Barker   Mr. Allen Roginsky
(301) 975-2911   (301) 975-3603
ebarker@nist.gov   roginsky@nist.gov

Internet Security

NIST continues to support the development and enhancement of key management standards for PKI. As part of that work, NIST has led the development of an update to RFC 2560, *the X.509 Internet Public Key Infrastructure Online Certificate Status Protocol (OCSP) in the Internet Engineering Task Force. OCSP* is a widely-used protocol for the distribution of certificate revocation status information. This update will address ambiguities in the protocol description that have created interoperability problems between some OCSP client and OCSP server implementations. NIST has also contributed editors to four other drafts related to PKI. Two of these drafts, which focus on encoding rules for public keys and digital signatures for some of the more advanced NIST-approved algorithms (e.g., elliptic curves and digital signatures with robust padding schemes), were published as RFCs: RFC 5756, *Updates for RSAES-OAEP and RSASSA-PSS Algorithm Parameters*, and RFC 5758, Internet X.509 *Public Key Infrastructure: Additional Algorithms and Identifiers for DSA and ECDSA*.

In collaboration with the Advanced Network Technologies Division, CSD supported the deployment of DNSSEC in the authoritative root zone of the Internet in July 2010. Our sister agency, the National Telecommunications and Information Administration (NTIA), led this effort in their role as the root zone administrator. CSD provided technical support, playing a pivotal role in the development of technical requirements and the review of processes and procedures subsequently proposed by the Internet Assigned Numbers Authority (IANA) functions contractor and the root zone distributor.

CSD continues its collaboration with the Advanced Network Technologies Division to support the development of security enhancements for routing protocols. The goal of this work is to develop protocols that allow for the validation of Internet routing information in order to prevent attacks against the infrastructure that are intended to misroute Internet traffic or cause denial of service. Other ongoing activities are focused on key management and cryptographic agility to support the authentication of routing components (e.g., to support the Border Gateway Protocol).

Contacts:

Mr. William Polk	Dr. David Cooper
(301) 975-3348	(301) 975-3194
william.polk@nist.gov	david.cooper@nist.gov

Quantum Computing

Quantum computing, which uses quantum mechanical phenomena to perform operations on data, has the potential to become a major disruptive technology affecting cryptography and cryptanalysis given the potential increase in computing speed and power over conventional transistor-based computing. While a scalable quantum computing architecture has not been built, the physics and mathematics governing what can be done by a quantum computer are fairly well understood, and several algorithms have already been written for a quantum computing platform. Two of these algorithms are specifically applicable to cryptanalysis. Grover's quantum algorithm for database search potentially gives a quadratic speedup to brute force cryptanalysis of block ciphers and hash functions. Grover's algorithm may, therefore, have a long-term effect on the necessary key lengths and digest sizes required for the secure operation of cryptographic protocols.

An even larger threat is presented by Shor's quantum algorithms for discrete logarithms and factorization. Given a quantum computer large enough to perform simple cryptographic operations, Shor's algorithm provides a practical computational mechanism for solving the two ostensibly hard problems that underlie all widely-used public key cryptographic primitives. In particular, all the digital signature algorithms and public key-based key establishment schemes that are currently approved by NIST would be rendered insecure by the presence of even a fairly primitive quantum computer.

While practical quantum computers are not expected to be built in the next decade or so, it seems inevitable that they will eventually be built. NIST is responding to this eventuality by researching cryptographic algorithms for public key-based key agreement and digital signatures that are not susceptible to cryptanalysis by quantum algorithms. In the event that such algorithms cannot be found, NIST intends to draft standards for computer security architectures that do not rely on public key cryptographic primitives. In addition, NIST will examine new approaches, such as quantum key distribution.

During FY2010, NIST planned a workshop, scheduled for early FY2011, with the Joint Quantum Institute on "From Quantum Information and Complexity to Post Quantum Information Security". NIST also sent representatives to the Third International Workshop on Post-quantum Cryptography in May 2010. Additionally, NIST CSD awarded research grants on post-quantum cryptography to researchers at the University of Illinois Chicago and the University of California Berkeley.

NIST will continue to study security technologies that may be resistant to attack by quantum computers, especially those that have generated some degree of commercial impact. If any of these technologies emerge as both commercially viable and widely trusted within the cryptographic community, NIST hopes to move towards standardization.

Contact:
Mr. Ray Perlner
(301) 975-3357
ray.perlner@nist.gov

Authentication

To support the Office of Management and Budget (OMB) Memorandum M-04-04, E-Authentication Guidance for Federal Agencies, NIST developed SP 800-63, *Electronic Authentication Guideline*. The OMB policy memorandum defines four levels of authentication in terms of assurance about the validity of an asserted identity. SP 800-63 gives technical requirements and examples of authentication technologies that work by making individuals demonstrate possession and control of a secret for each of the four levels.

NIST is now in the process of updating and revising SP 800-63, and has issued two drafts. Extensive comments have been received that reflect the extent to which SP 800-63 has been adopted by many non-federal users and indicate a number of applications that were not anticipated in the original version or in the draft. The most difficult issues involve proposed new methods for reaching the highest authentication level, with current technologies. Both comments on the second draft, along with additional comments from the OpenID consortium and the Federal CIO Council's Citizen Outreach Focus Group raised concerns with the password entropy and identity proofing requirements. These concerns are being addressed in a third draft expected in early FY2011, leading to final publication later in the fiscal year.

Contacts:

Mr. William Polk	Mr. Ray Perlner
(301) 975-3348	(301) 975-3357
william.polk@nist.gov	ray.perlner@nist.gov

Security Aspects of Electronic Voting

In 2002, Congress passed the Help America Vote Act (HAVA) to encourage the upgrade of voting equipment across the United States. HAVA established the Election Assistance Commission (EAC) and the Technical Guidelines Development Committee (TGDC), chaired by the Director of NIST. HAVA calls on NIST to provide technical support to the EAC and TGDC in efforts related to human factors, security, and laboratory accreditation. As part of NIST's efforts led by the Software and Systems Division of ITL, CSD supports the activities of the EAC and the TGDC related to voting equipment security.

In the past year, NIST supported the efforts of the EAC and Federal Voting Assistance Program (FVAP) of the Department of Defense to improve the voting process for citizens under the Uniformed and Overseas Citizens Voting Act (UOCAVA) by leveraging electronic technologies. This work included the development of project plans and roadmaps for how NIST, EAC, and FVAP work towards remote electronic absentee voting systems; participation in the development of testable pilot requirements for kiosk-based Internet voting systems; organization and hosting of the UOCAVA Remote Voting System Workshop and the development of the following documents: "IT Security Best Practices for UOCAVA Supporting Voting Systems," "Security Best Practices for the Electronic Distribution of Election Materials" and "Security Considerations for Remote Electronic UOCAVA Voting".

In addition, NIST supported the EAC in updating the Voluntary Voting System Guidelines (VVSG) 1.1, by assisting the EAC with resolutions to public comments and providing test suites for the updated security requirements. NIST also organized and held the End-To-End Voting System Workshop to investigate the viability of using these novel voting systems for large-scale elections.

In FY2011, NIST will continue to support the efforts of the EAC and FVAP to improve the voting process for UOCAVA voters. NIST will work with the UOCAVA Working Group of the TGDC to develop high-level, goal-oriented requirements for remote electronic absentee UOCAVA voting systems, and to identify possible pilot voting systems for the 2012 election. NIST will continue to conduct research on threats to voting systems and innovative voting system architectures. In addition, NIST will support the NIST National Voluntary Laboratory Accreditation Program (NVLAP) efforts to accredit voting system test laboratories and host the TGDC plenary meetings. NIST plans to engage voting system manufacturers, voting system test laboratories, state election officials, and the academic community in exploring ways to increase voting system security and transparency.

http://vote.nist.gov/
Contacts:
Dr. Nelson Hastings   Mr. Andrew Regenscheid
(301) 975-5237   (301) 975-5155
nelson.hastings@nist.gov   andrew.regenscheid@nist.gov

Development of Federal Information Processing Standards (FIPS) 140-3, Security Requirements for Cryptographic Modules

FIPS 140-3 (Draft), *Security Requirements for Cryptographic Modules,* provides four increasing qualitative levels of security that are intended to cover a wide range of potential applications and environments. The security requirements cover areas related to the secure design and implementation of a cryptographic module. These areas include cryptographic module specification; cryptographic module physical ports and logical interfaces; roles, authentication, and services; software security; operational environment; physical security; physical security – non-invasive attacks; sensitive security parameter management; self-tests; life-cycle assurance; and mitigation of other attacks. The standard provides users with a specification of security features that are required at each of four security levels, flexibility in choosing security requirements, a guide to ensuring that the cryptographic modules incorporate necessary security features, and the assurance that the modules are compliant with cryptography-based standards.

The FIPS 140-3 draft is a result of the reexamination and reaffirmation of the current standard, FIPS 140-2. The draft standard adds new security requirements on cryptographic modules to reflect the latest advances in technology and security, and to mirror other new or updated standards published by NIST in the area of cryptography and key management. Additionally, software and firmware requirements are specifically addressed. Also a new section specifying requirements to protect against non-invasive attacks is provided.

The development of FIPS 140-3 started in 2005 and relied on the preliminary inputs provided by users, laboratories, and vendors during the September 2004 NIST-CSE Cryptographic Module Validation Symposium and the September 2005 NIST-CSE Physical Security Workshop. In 2007, the first draft of the standard was released for public comment, and NIST received over 1,200 comments, which were thoroughly reviewed and discussed, and the working group's resolutions were implemented in the second draft of the standard. In December 2009; the second draft of the standard was released for public comment, and NIST received over 900 comments. NIST's goal is to release the final standard in FY2011.

Contact:
Dr. Michaela Iorga
(301) 975-8431
michaela.iorga@nist.go

Cryptographic Technology (CT) Group Guidelines and Documents

CT's guidelines and documents along with the abstracts to these documents can be found in the Publications section on page 51-60.

Systems and Emerging Technologies Security Research Group

STRATEGIC GOAL

Devise advanced security methods, tools, and guidelines through conducting near term and midterm security research.

Overview

In our security research, we focus on identifying emerging technologies and developing security solutions that will have a high impact on the critical information infrastructure. We conduct research and development on behalf of government and industry from the earliest stages of technology development through proof-of-concept, reference and prototype implementations, and demonstrations. We work to transfer new technologies to industry, to produce new standards, and to develop tests, test methodologies, and assurance methods.

To keep pace with the rate of change in emerging technologies, we conduct a large amount of research in existing and emerging technology areas. Some of the many topics we research include smart card infrastructure and security, wireless and mobile device security, security automation, digital forensics tools and methods, access control and authorization management, internet protocol (IP) security, cloud computing, application security for handheld devices, and vulnerability analysis. Our research helps to fulfill specific needs of the federal government for information security methods which are not easily available.

We collaborate extensively with government, academia, and private sector entities. In the past year, collaborations have included the National Security Agency, the Department of Defense, the Defense Advanced Research Projects Agency, the Department of Justice, the University of Maryland, George Mason University, Rutgers University, Purdue University, George Washington University, the University of Maryland-Baltimore County, Columbia University, Microsoft Corporation, Sun Microsystems, the Boeing Company, Intel Corporation, Lucent Technologies, Oracle Corporation, and MITRE.

Identity Management Systems

Personal Identity Verification (PIV)

In response to Homeland Security Presidential Directive 12 (HSPD-12), Policy for a Common Identification Standard for Federal Employees and Contractors, Federal Information Processing Standard (FIPS) 201, *Personal Identity Verification (PIV) of Federal Employees and Contractors*, was developed and was approved by the Secretary of Commerce in February 2005. HSPD-12 calls for the creation of a new identity credential for federal employees and contractors. FIPS 201 is the technical specification of both the new identity credential and the PIV system that produces, manages, and uses the credential. According to the Office of Management and Budget (OMB), as of June 2010; approximately 4 million federal employees and contractors (68 percent of the federal workforce) have been issued their PIV cards. This work is done in collaboration with the Cryptographic Technologies Group.

CSD activities in FY2010 directly supported the increase in operational use of the identity credential by federal agencies. To achieve this level of use, CSD:

- Provided assistance to federal departments and agencies and their suppliers;

- Maintained the stability of and eased implementation of FIPS 201-1 by limiting modifications to the supporting Special Publications (SP); changes were limited to those committed to and scheduled in previous years, a small number of necessary, backward-compatible process and technical improvements (detailed below), and editorial improvements for clarity.

SP 800-73-3 Interfaces for Personal Identity Verification

In February 2010, we released the third revision of SP 800-73, *Interfaces for Personal Identity Verification*. This revision features technical improvements and clarifications for PIV cards and related PIV systems such as:

1) Encryption Key History Management - to enable on-card retention of retired Key Management keys and corresponding X.509 certificates for the purpose of deriving or decrypting data encryption keys with the help of retired Key Management key(s);

2) Key Establishment – to clarify the use of the Elliptic Curve Diffie-Hellman key establishment scheme with the Key Management key, as specified in SP 800-78-2; and

3) Non-Federal Issuer (NFI) provisions – to enable the use of PIV Compatible (PIV-C) and PIV Interoperable (PIV-I) cards for NFI

credentials, in accordance with the Federal CIO Council's NFI card specifications.

SP 800-78-2 Cryptographic Algorithms and Key Sizes for Personal Identity Verification

Also in February 2010, we released the second revision of SP 800-78, *Cryptographic Algorithms and Key Sizes for Personal Identity Verification (PIV)*. The document has been modified:

1) To re-align with the recently published FIPS 186-3, *Digital Signature Standard (DSS)*; and

2) To eliminate a redundant encryption mode for symmetric PIV authentication protocols.

SP 800-85A-2 PIV Card Application and Middleware Interface Test Guidelines (SP 800-73-3 Compliance)

In July 2010, the second revision of SP 800-85A, *PIV Card Application and Middleware Interface Test Guidelines (SP800-73-3 Compliance)* was published. This document provides Derived Test Requirements (DTR) and Test Assertions (TA) for testing the PIV Middleware, and the PIV Card Application interfaces for conformance to specifications in SP 800-73-3.

The year 2010 marks the fifth anniversary of the publication of FIPS 201. According to FIPS 201, the five year mark is the year when the review and possible revision of the standard are required to maintain its adequacy and ability to adapt to advancements and innovations in science and technology. Over the past five years, NIST has received numerous change requests for FIPS 201. In 2010, we reviewed these requests and began the approval process for a revision. As a first step, NIST held a business requirements meeting for federal departments and agencies to validate the change requests against current business requirements and to begin gathering new or changed business requirements.

In 2011, as a result, we will be focusing on the revision of FIPS 201. Upon approval of the revision, a Federal Register Notice will be published notifying the public of the FIPS 201 revision process.

---

http://csrc.nist.gov/groups/SNS/piv
Contacts:
Mr. William I. MacGregor   Ms. Hildegard Ferraiolo
(301) 975-8721   (301) 975-6972
william.macgregor@nist.gov   hildegard.ferraiolo@nist. gov

NIST Personal Identity Verification Program (NPIVP)

The objective of the NIST Personal Identity Verification Program (NPIVP) is to validate Personal Identity Verification (PIV) components for conformance to specifications in FIPS 201 and its companion documents. The two PIV components that come under the scope of NPIVP are PIV Smart Card Application and PIV Middleware. All of the tests under NPVIP are handled by third-party laboratories that are accredited as Cryptographic and Security and Testing (CST) Laboratories by the National Voluntary Laboratory Accreditation Program (NVLAP) and are called accredited NPIVP test facilities. As of September 2010, there are nine such facilities.

In prior years, CSD published SP 800-85A, *PIV Card Application and Middleware Interface Test Guidelines*, to facilitate development of PIV Smart Card Application and PIV Middleware that conform to interface specifications in SP 800-73, *Interfaces for Personal Identity Verification*. We also developed an integrated toolkit called "PIV Interface Test Runner" for conducting tests on both PIV Card Application and PIV Middleware products, and provided the toolkit to accredited NPIVP test facilities.

In FY2010, the third edition of SP 800-73 (numbered as SP 800-73-3), was published. After SP 800-73-3 was finalized, we updated SP 800-85A-1, *PIV Card Application and Middleware Interface Test Guidelines*, to provide test guidelines that align with SP 800-73-3. After a public comment period and resolution of received comments, the final publication of SP 800-85A-2 was released in July 2010.

With the release of SP 800-73-3, NPIVP identified the necessary updates for the PIV Interface Test Runner to align with SP 800-73-3 and the revised PIV card interface test guidelines in SP 800-85A-2. The PIV Interface Test Runner is in the process of being updated to perform additional tests needed for SP 800-73-3 compliance and will be made available to accredited NPIVP test facilities in the first quarter of FY2011. With the introduction of the new Test Runner, the NPIVP test facilities will base all future evaluations of PIV Card application and PIV Middleware products on the new PIV Interface Test Runner.

With the release of SP 800-78-2, *Cryptographic Algorithms and Key Sizes for Personal Identity Verification*, in 2005 and continuing with subsequent released revisions, dates were established for discontinuing the use of certain cryptographic algorithms in the PIV System and PIV Cards. By the beginning of January 1, 2011, for example, the 2 Key Triple DES algorithms (2TDEA) for the PIV card's optional Card Authentication Key (CAK) was discontinued. This action was necessary to ensure adequate cryptographic strength for the PIV card. Instead of 2TDEA, higher strength cryptographic algorithms are specified in SP 800-78-2, such as 3 Key Triple DES algorithms (3TDEA), AES 128 and other. In anticipation of the discontinuation of the 2TDEA for the affected PIV cards, NPIVP coordinated the upgrade to higher strength CAK and CMK, and provided re-validation guidelines for affected client products. Fortunately, no PIV Card Application products were affected by the discontinuation of 2 Key Triple DES, since validated PIV cards already had the capability to provide higher cryptographic strength for the CAK and CMK.

In FY2010, four more PIV Card application products were validated and certificates issued, bringing the total number of NPIVP-validated PIV Card Application products to 21. One more PIV Middleware products was validated and issued certificates, bringing the total number of NPIVP-validated PIV Middleware products to 12.

http://csrc.nist.gov/groups/SNS/piv/npivp
Contacts:

Dr. Ramaswamy Chandramouli
(301) 975-5013
mouli@nist.gov

Ms. Hildegard Ferraiolo
(301) 975-6972
hildegard.ferraiolo@nist.gov

Conformance Tests for Transportation Worker Identification Credential (TWIC) Specifications

The Department of Homeland Security (DHS) has asked NIST and CSD to assist with their Transportation Worker Identification Credential (TWIC) specifications. The TWIC program is under the provisions of the Maritime Transportation Security Act (MTSA) and is a joint initiative of the Transportation Security Administration (TSA) and the U.S. Coast Guard, both under DHS. TWIC is a common identification credential for all personnel requiring unescorted access to secure areas of MTSA-regulated facilities and vessels, and all mariners must hold Coast Guard-issued credentials. TSA issued workers a tamper-resistant "Smart Card" containing the worker's biometric (finger print template) to allow for a positive link between the card it self and the individual. The TSA also has a requirement to establish a process to qualify products and to maintain a Qualified Products List (QPL) for use within the TWIC program.

DHS has asked CSD to assist with the establishment of a conformity assessment framework in support of a QPL for identity and privilege credential products, to be managed by TSA. Additionally, CSD is assisting with the establishment of a testing regime for the qualifying products for conformity to specified standards and TSA specifications. CSD's wealth of experience with the Cryptographic Module Validation Program (CMVP), smart card technology, and specific experience with the Personal Identity Verification (PIV) card validation program, makes CSD uniquely qualified to assist TSA in establishing a conformity assessment program and a QPL for the TWIC Program.

In FY2010, CSD set the framework for the conformity assessment regime for TWIC readers and for the QPL for the credential readers that successfully passed the conformity tests and satisfy all TWIC requirements. As part of this work, the following documents have been developed:

- QPL's Administrative Manual addressing QPL Owner's Quality Manual, Product Submission Procedures, Product Approval Procedures, etc.;

- Fixed Reader Approval Procedure document;

- Portable Reader Approval Procedure document;

- Derived Test Requirements document;

- Fixed Reader Test Procedures document;

- Portable Reader Test Procedures document; and

- NVLAP HB 150-17 – TWIC Program pertaining sections.

We are currently developing, in collaboration with our partners, the conformity assessment testing suit for credential readers. CSD will continue to support DHS/TSA's efforts by assisting TSA in launching and managing the Conformity Assessment Program and the QPL

Contact:
Ms. Michaela Iorga
(301) 975-8431
michaela.iorga@nist.gov

Identity Credential Smart Card Interoperability: ISO/IEC 24727 Identification Cards-Integrated Circuit Cards Programming Interfaces

According to recent reports, identity theft continues to be a growing problem. Solutions providing secure and strongly authenticated identity credentials are increasingly important for safeguarding personal information and protecting the integrity of IT systems. A smart card coupled with security protections provides an example of the necessary elements of such a solution. A smart card can provide cryptographic mechanisms, store biometrics and keys, support interoperability, and address privacy considerations. Technological solutions for identity credentials should increase the reliability of information, improve consumer/user trust and protect privacy, while enabling interoperable applications. An example of such a credential is the HSPD-12 PIV smart card.

The United States has led international efforts to address interoperability limitations and the lack of normative authentication mechanisms for improving the security and interoperability of identity management systems. In FY2010, these efforts resulted in a new standard, International Organization for Standardization/ International Electrotechnical Commission (ISO/IEC) 24727, *Identification Cards – Integrated Circuit Cards Programming Interfaces*. This multipart standard addresses existing ambiguities in current standards that challenge interoperability. In addition, it introduces much needed application programming interfaces and normative processes for identification, authentication, and signature services.

ISO/IEC 24727 established the architecture required to develop secure and interoperable frameworks for smart card technology based identity credentials. It enables interoperable and interchangeable smart card systems, eliminating consumer reliance on proprietary-based solutions historically provided by industry. Existing standards provide the consumer a great degree of flexibility, which can introduce challenges to achieving interoperable solutions for identity credentials, card readers, and card applications. ISO/IEC 24727 builds on these standards, fine-tuning them to improve interoperability and addressing areas that were lacking, such as a normative authentication protocols and identification, authentication, and signature services. With innovation as a central theme of our standards activities, this body of international work was developed to enable technological choices for identity management applications of the future, to include USB tokens, mobile devices, and cloud applications.

Furthering the development of formally recognized international standards through collaborative efforts with public and private sectors will support organizations in providing an interoperable and secure method for interagency use of smart card technology, in particular for identity management activities.

This standard (ISO/IEC 24727) has been publicly adopted by the European community for the European Union Citizens Card, by Germany for the German health card, and by Queensland, Australia for their next generation driver's license. We continue to work with the U.S. national standards committees to ensure compatibility with federal credentials and to address the needs of non-federal communities.

Contact:
Mr. Sal Francomacaro
(301) 975-6414
salfra@nist.gov

Biometric Standards and Conformity Assessment Activities

Biometric technologies are currently required in many public and private sector applications worldwide to authenticate an individual's identity, secure national borders and restrict access to secure sites including buildings and computer networks. Biometrics provide for secure transactions, positive identification, and augmentation to human judgment. Use of biometrics is being considered by financial institutions, the healthcare industry, and in educational applications. Consumer uses are also expected to significantly increase for personal security and convenience in home automation and security systems, and in the retail, gaming and hospitality industries. These many varied uses require the development of open standards to maintain interoperability and encourage continued adoption.

The NIST Biometrics program supports the development of voluntary standards for biometrics, and responds to government, industry and market demands for open systems standards by:

- Accelerating development of formal national and international biometric standards and associated conformity assessment;

- Educating users on the capability of standards-based open systems solutions;

- Promoting standards adoption;

- Developing conformance test architectures and test tools to test implementations of these standards;

- Supporting harmonization of biometric, tokens and security standards; and

- Addressing the use of biometric-based solutions for ID Management applications.

Currently, NIST staff leads both the national and international biometric standards bodies and participates in a number of biometric standards development projects. Our experts work in close collaboration with the NIST Information Access Division biometric experts and the ITL Standards Liaison. Our efforts have become a major catalyst for biometric standardization and adoption of biometric standards.

In FY2010, NIST continued to work in close partnership with government agencies, industry, and academic institutions to develop formal national and international biometric standards. NIST actively

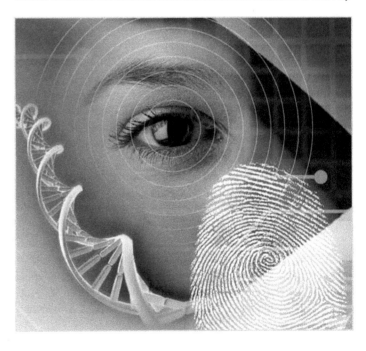

participated in the National Science and Technology Council Subcommittee on Biometrics and Identity Management and its Standards and Conformity Assessment Working Group. Additionally, we participated in the Department of Homeland Security Biometrics Working Group, the Department of Defense Biometrics Identity Management Agency Biometric Standards Working Group and other government groups.

Currently, biometric base standards for data interchange and technical interfaces do not provide specific conditions for demonstrating that products implementing the standards meet all of the technical requirements. Conformance testing to biometric standards captures the technical description of a specification and measures whether a product's implementation faithfully implements the specification. A conformance test suite is test software that is used to ascertain such conformance. CSD continues to actively contribute to the development of technical interface standards; biometric data interchange format standards, and biometric conformance testing methodology standards. We also continued to develop conformance test architectures and conformance test suites that support product developers, end users, and testing laboratories.

In August 2010, we released Beta 2.0 of an Advanced Conformance Test Architecture (CTA) that supports conformance test suites designed to test implementations of biometric data interchange data formats, as well as the three components of Biometric Information Records conforming to Common Biometric Exchange Framework Format standards. CTA Beta 2.0 incorporates features designed to improve the confidence and reliability of test results and the usability of the test tools. Software development testing approaches incorporated in this CTA version allow for the potential of cleaner, more trustworthy code. At the same time, we released conformance test suites[2] designed to test implementations of four American National Standard data interchange formats[3]. The release incorporates features commonly found in commercially available software (e.g., installer/uninstaller, detailed context-sensitive help). The CTA was released with two documents: the Overview and a detailed User Guide. The conformance testing suites were released with one document each and associated sample data.

The CTA Beta 2.0 key features include:

- Modularity: the CTA is a set of individual components. Each component was independently developed and tested. This approach allows for faster upgrades;

- Dynamically-Loaded Modules: conformance test suite modules, if present, are automatically loaded at runtime. They are developed and deployed without changing any other CTA software;

- Binary Data is in Context: when the CTA processes binary data it places the data into an array of field data structures. A test suite module's complexity is greatly reduced by the pre-

parsed arrays of fields;

- Structure Testing by Field Groups: the test suite modules implement testing of groups of fields (e.g., data format record header, finger minutiae header). This approach reduces development and testing complexity;

- Manifest or Decode-based Testing: when the format of a binary implementation is known it can be described to the test suite via an XML "Manifest". When the data structure is not known the test suite decodes the input data and develops a "Manifest";

- Powerful Test Case Features: they ensure the correct operation of the test modules and test that the modules perform correctly with a wide variety of data; and

- XML Output: output results can be transformed into any custom format desired (HTML, text, comma separated values, database queries, etc.) through an XSLT Transformation. Three XSLT report transformations are included.

Planned work for FY2011 includes development of conformance test suites to test implementations of selected first and second generation international biometric data interchange formats as well as selected ANSI/NIST-ITL 1-2007 Record Types[4]. Contributions towards the development of the 2011 version of ANSI/NIST ITL standard are also planned. Our current strategy includes simultaneous development of the conformance test suites for the selected standards as these standards are being developed (making adjustments as needed) so that the suites are available at the time of publication of the standards or soon thereafter.

Changes to the architecture leading towards the development of CTA Beta 3.0 are also planned. Such changes may include the re-development of some of the Graphical User Interfaces to accommodate the diverse types of test suites planned (binary as well as tag-based testing) and to improve the usability of the tools. Some of the features also being researched and/or implemented are providing for full web services support and the development of a test

[2] The CTA/CTS Download web page is http://www.nist.gov/itl/csd/biometrics/biocta_download.cfm. The web page can be also reached from NIST/ITL Biometric Resource Center http://www.nist.gov/biometrics under **ITL Computer Security Division (CSD)/Systems and Emerging Technologies Security Research Group** - "Standards and Related Technical Developments" http://www.nist.gov/itl/csd/biometrics/csdbiomstds.cfm.

[3] The released CTSs were developed to test implementations of four published American National Standards: ANSI INCITS 378-2004 and 2009 (Finger Minutiae Format for Data Interchange) and ANSI INCITS 381-2004 and 2009 (Information Technology - Finger Image-Based Data Interchange Format).

[4]This work is sponsored, in part, by DHS/US-VISIT.

suite developer's kit to promote third-party development of modules that can be incorporated into the architecture. Research is also planned on the need for the development of additional test suites for implementations of new biometric technical interface standards being developed internationally.

The Biometric Consortium (the Consortium), co-chaired by NIST and the National Security Agency (NSA), serves as a focal point for research, development, testing, evaluation, and application of biometric-based personal identification/verification technology. The Consortium's primary activity is an annual conference, which enables federal government participants to engage in exchanges with national and international participants on topics such as biometric technologies for defense, homeland security, identity management, border crossing and electronic commerce. This conference is considered "the federal government's major outreach effort each year."[5]

The 2010 conference, co-sponsored by NIST, NSA, the Departments of Homeland Security and Defense, Federal Bureau of Investigation, the National Institute of Justice, the General Services Administration, and the Armed Forces Communications and Electronics Association, was held September 21-23, 2010. The conference addressed the important role that biometrics can play in the identification and verification of individuals in government and commercial applications worldwide. This very successful event attracted about 1,800 attendees including over 130 national and international speakers from industry, government and academia.

Sessions included planned and current government initiatives and programs, technology innovations (including a special session on Rapid DNA), biometric standards and the latest trends in biometrics research, development and applications of biometric technologies as well commercial applications in the United States and abroad. Biometrics in relation with identity and security was also addressed. Presentations as well as a video sent by The Honorable Janet Napolitano, U.S. Secretary of the Department of Homeland Security, are available at: http://www.biometrics.org/bc2010/program.pdf.

---

http://www.nist.gov/biometrics
Contact:
Mr. Fernando Podio
(301) 975-2947
fernando.podio@nist.gov

Access Control – Information Sharing Environment

Information flow within an organization may be controlled mostly by operational and managerial procedures. However, when information is requested by another entity, organizations may avoid sharing information because they aren't sure what access rules should be applied. This activity explores possible protections for privacy and accountability, and provides a mean to give the right information to authorized users at the right time while complying with and enforcing federal, state, local or tribal security and privacy policies.

The activity involves applying electronic security and privacy policy access controls in an information sharing environment such as the Privilege Management Project for Fusion Centers which is based on the National Information Exchange Model (NIEM). This activity will develop the supporting standards and guidance for reference implementations. A pilot will be built upon the multi-year Global Federated Identity and Privilege Management (GFIPM) work to help NIEM leap forward in supporting institutionalized secure information sharing, and to provide critical support for Identity and Authorization Management challenges within the Information Sharing Environment.

We developed a prototype Policy Evaluation Testbed (PET) for the Director of National Intelligence (DNI) Privilege Management Pilot project. The PET addresses the concerns of law enforcement officials, Fusion Center analysts, and privacy advocates by enabling sharing of more information in a timely manner with enforceable and auditable access policies. This year, we added more flexible and capable functions in the test bed including[6]:

- Enhanced Policy Evaluation Point (PEP) function, which can resolve policy conflicts between federal and state policies;

- More complex policy scenarios for the PET demonstration;

- Applied Access Control Protocol Tool (ACPT) for rule composing, property verification, policy combination, and eXtensible Access Control Markup Language (XACML) policy generation for PET samples; and

- Global Attribute Framework (GAF) with demonstration scenarios that provide the portability for specifying privacy rules of various access control domains;

To increase the visibility and use of the test bed, we wrote a report, which describes the lesson learned, and suggestions for future work. We also presented the PET and GAF systems to many interested agencies and organizations.

Contacts:
Dr. Vincent Hu
(301) 975-4975
vhu@nist.gov

Dr. Stephen Quirolgico
(301) 975-8246
stephen.quirolgico@nist.gov

Dr. Tom Karygiannis
(301) 975-4782
tom.karygiannis@nist.gov

[5] "Biometrics in Government Post 9-11"

[6] The Global Federated Identity and Privilege Management (GFIPM) framework provides the justice community and partner organizations with a standards-based approach for implementing federated identity. http://www.it.ojp.gov/gfipm

Access Control and Privilege Management Research

With the advance of current computing technologies and the multifaceted environments the technologies are applied to, security issues such as situation awareness, trust management, privacy control for access control and privilege management systems are becoming more complex. However, the research available on these topics is generally targeted to a specific system, is incomplete, or makes assumptions, or is ambiguous regarding critical elements. Thus, practical and conceptual general guidance for these topics is needed.

During FY2010, we researched trust management using the Global Attribute Framework for distributed information shared environments with different domains of subjects and resources. We also investigated the capability of attribute specification for access control mechanisms; the result was published in the paper "Specification of Attribute Relations for Access Control Policies and Constraints Using Policy Machine" that was submitted for the Sixth International Conference on Information Assurance and Security held in Atlanta, Georgia in August, 2010.

In FY2011, we will continue our investigation on trust management frameworks and the situation awareness feature of access control mechanisms. We plan to develop an evaluation metric for access control mechanisms. The evaluation metric will define and describe access control properties, which will then be used in the metric as factors for the evaluation or comparison of access control mechanisms/products. We expect that this project will:

- Promote (or accelerate) the adoption of community computing that utilizes the power of shared resources and common trust management schemes;

- Provide a standard evaluation metric in evaluating or comparing access control mechanisms for implementing access control applications;

- Increase security and safety of static (connected) distributed systems by applying the testing and verification tool for the access control polices; and

- Assist system architects, security administrators, and security managers whose expertise is related to access control or privilege policy in managing their systems, and in learning the limitations and practical approaches for their applications.

Contacts:

Dr. Vincent Hu   Mr. David Ferraiolo
(301) 975-4975   (301) 975-3046
vhu@nist.gov   david.ferraiolo@nist.gov

Mr. Rick Kuhn
(301) 975-3337
kuhn@nist.gov

Automated Combinatorial Testing for Software (ACTS)

NIST research suggests that software faults are triggered by only a few interacting variables. This idea has important implications for testing. If all faults in a system can be triggered by a combination of n or fewer parameters (where n is the number of parameters), then testing all n-way combinations of parameters can provide high confidence that nearly all faults have been discovered. For example, if we know from historical failure data that failures for a particular application never involve more than four parameters, then testing all 4-way or 5-way combinations of parameters gives strong confidence that flaws will be found in testing.

We are working with the University of Texas, Arlington on a project initiated in 2006, to take advantage of this empirical observation by developing software test methods and tools that can test all n-way combinations of parameter values. The methods have been demonstrated in a proof-of-concept study and are being further developed through application to real-world projects at NIST and elsewhere.

This work uses two relatively recent advances in software engineering-algorithms for efficiently generating covering arrays and automated generation of test oracles using model checking. Covering arrays are test data sets that cover all n-way combinations of parameter values. Pairwise (all pairs of values) testing has been popular for some time, but our research indicates that pairwise testing is not sufficient for high assurance software. Model checking technology enables the construction of the results expected from a test case by exploring all states of a mathematical model of the system being tested. Tools developed in this project will have applications in high assurance software, safety and security, and combinatorial testing.

Accomplishments for FY2010 include the following:

- Released a comprehensive tutorial on combinatorial testing which consolidates research in the field from NIST and others, making it accessible in a single publication suitable for use by developers or in an undergraduate or graduate computer science program;

- Initiated a Cooperative Research and Development Agreement with Lockheed Martin Corporation, to investigate the application of combinatorial methods to a variety of software testing problems;

- Developed, jointly with the U.S. Air Force, a combinatorial approach and algorithm for testing event sequences. The method has been applied successfully to interoperability testing for a mission-critical system;

- Released a new version of the automated combinatorial testing tool ACTS+, with improved Graphic User Interface (GUI) and constraint handling. The tool has now been acquired by more than 400 organizations in IT, finance, defense, and many other industries;

- Published, jointly with Johns Hopkins University Applied Physics Laboratory, a method for analyzing combinatorial state-space coverage of software tests, with application to spacecraft tests;

- Developed, jointly with North Carolina State University, a tool for testing access control systems using combinatorial methods; and

- Presented lectures on combinatorial testing to universities and government agencies.

Plans for FY2011 include cooperative work with industry and government agencies to investigate the effectiveness of combinatorial testing for large systems; development of methods and tools for fault location; application of combinatorial methods to interoperability testing, buffer overflow detection, and XACML access control; extension of event sequence covering array algorithm to include constraints, and development of lecture and course material to transfer this technology to industry.

---

http://csrc.nist.gov/acts
Contacts:

Mr. Rick Kuhn	Dr. Raghu Kacker
(301) 975-3337	Mathematical and Computational
kuhn@nist.gov	Sciences Division
	(301) 975-2109
	raghu.kacker@nist.gov

Conformance Verification for Access Control Policies

Access control systems are among the most critical network security components. Faulty policies, misconfigurations, or flaws in software implementation can result in serious vulnerabilities. The specification of access control policies is often a challenging problem. Often a system's privacy and security are compromised due to the misconfiguration of access control policies instead of the failure of cryptographic primitives or protocols. This problem becomes increasingly severe as software systems become more and more complex, and are deployed to manage a large amount of sensitive information and resources organized into sophisticated structures. Identifying discrepancies between policy specifications and their properties (intended function) are crucial because correct implementation and enforcement of policies by applications is based on the premise that the policy specifications are correct. As a result, policy specifications must undergo rigorous verification and validation through systematic testing to ensure that the policy specifications truly encapsulate the desires of the policy authors.

To formally and precisely capture the security properties that access control should adhere to, access control models are usually written, bridging the rather wide gap in abstraction between policy and mechanism. Thus, an access control model provides unambiguous

and precise expression as well as reference for design and implementation of security requirements. Techniques are required for verifying whether an access control model is correctly expressed in the access controls policies and whether the properties are satisfied in the model. In practice, the same access control policies may express multiple access control models or express a single model in addition to extra access control constraints outside of the model. Ensuring the conformance of access control models and policies is a non-trivial and critical task.

Started from 2009, we have developed a prototype system -- Access Control Property Tool (ACPT), which allows a user to compose, verify, test and generate access control policies. During FY2010, we added more model templates and XACML generating capability in the tool. We also performed testing of the tool in an information sharing environment, as well as resolving issues in specifying and combining access control rules. We have included this work in publications to increase familiarity and use.

1. "Model Checking for Verification of Mandatory Access Control Models and Properties", Int'l Journal of Software Engineering and Knowledge Engineering (IJSEKE) to be published in regular issue volume 21, May 2011;

2. "Mining Likely Properties of Access Control Policies via Association Rule Mining", proceedings of the 24th Annual IFIP WG 11.3 Working Conference on Data and Applications Security (DBSec 2010), Rome, Italy, June 2010; and

3. "Specification of Attribute Relations for Access Control Policies and Constraints Using Policy Machine", proceeding p32-35, the "Sixth International Conference on Information Assurance and Security" (IAS 2010). Atlanta, US, Aug, 23-25, 2010.

In FY2011, in addition to continuing research, we will enhance the capability of ACPT adding flexible states and classes for Workflow and Multilevel access control models, as well as performing Alpha and Beta testing for the tool. We also plan to make ACPT available from the CSD website for public download.

This project is expected to:

- Provide generic paradigm and framework of access control model/property conformance testing;

- Provide templates for specifying access control rules in popular access control models such as Attribute Based, Multilevel, and Workflow models;

- Provide tools or services for checking the security and safety of access control implementation, policy combination, and XACML policy generation;

- Promote (or accelerate) the adoption of combinatorial testing for large system (such as access control system) testing; and

- Assist system architects, security administrators, and security managers whose expertise is related to access control in managing their systems, and to learn the limitations and practical approaches for their applications.

Contacts:

Dr. Vincent Hu
(301) 975-4975
vhu@nist.gov

Mr. Rick Kuhn
(301) 975-3337
kuhn@nist.gov

Forensics for Web Services

Web services are becoming a popular way to design and implement a Service Oriented Architecture (SOA) in areas such as financial, government and military applications. Web services enable a seamless integration of different systems over the Internet using choreographies, orchestrations, and dynamic invocations. Web services based on the eXtensible Markup Language (XML), Simple Object Access Protocol (SOAP), and related open standards, deployed in SOA, allow data and applications to interact without human intervention through dynamic ad hoc connections.

The security challenges presented by the Web services approach are formidable. Many of the features that make Web services attractive, including greater accessibility of data, dynamic application-to-application connections, and relative autonomy (lack of human intervention) are at odds with traditional security models and controls. Compositions of new services create service interdependencies that can be misused for monetary or other gains. When a misuse is reported, investigators have to navigate through a collection of logs to recreate the attack. In order to facilitate that task, we are investigating techniques for forensics on web services (FWS), a specialized web service that when used would securely maintain transactional records between web services. These secure records can be re-linked to reproduce the transactional history by an independent agency. In FY2010, we enhanced our techniques for different kinds of attacks (such as cross site scripting). We also published our results in NISTIR 7559, *Forensic Web Services*.

Contact:
Dr. Anoop Singhal
(301) 975-4432
anoop.singhal@nist.gov

Mobile Handheld Device Security and Forensics

Nearly everyone in the United States today has a cell phone or other mobile handheld device for personal and professional communications. Mobile devices allow users to place calls; perform texting; access multimedia; use instant messaging; exchange email; browse the Web; manage address book and calendar entries; capture photos and videos; and create, edit, and read digital documents. The amount of information that accumulates on a device over time is often significant and may contain private or organizational information that needs to be protected from intruders, or, in a security incident or crime investigation, needs to be recovered as evidence. For these reasons, mobile handheld devices are a rapidly growing area of computer security and forensics. The focus of the mobile security and forensics project is twofold:

- To improve the security of mobile devices; and

- To improve the state-of-the-art of mobile device forensics.

Although mobile handheld devices in many ways approach the functionality of desktop computers, their organization and operation are quite different in certain areas. For example, most cell phones do not contain a hard drive and rely instead on flash memory for persistent storage. These devices are also generally treated more as fixed appliances with a limited set of functions than as general-purpose systems with the capability for expansion. In addition, no single operating system dominates cell phones. Such differences make the application of traditional computer security and forensic techniques difficult. In October, 2009, a complete methodology for device population was finalized and documented in NISTIR 7617, *Mobile Forensic Reference Materials: A Methodology and Reification*. The report also includes test results from applying the methodology to assess popular forensic tools.

To better illustrate the concept, an open source application, called SIMfill and a companion set of test data were developed that embody the methodology for certain classes of cell phone equipment. A new release of the distribution package was issued in FY2010. Detailed documentation of the release was published in February, 2010 in NISTIR 7658, *Guide to SIMfill Use and Development*. The report explains how organizations can revise and extend both the application and dataset to suit their particular needs. The distribution package and the reports can be found at the project website. Potential follow-on work includes investigating ways to improve the reference test data, using techniques such as fuzzing and combinatorial test generation, and extending the application to other devices. The intended audience for these products ranges broadly from computer response team members, to organizational security officials, to law enforcement.

http://csrc.nist.gov/groups/SNS/mobile_security/
Contact:
Mr. Wayne Jansen
(301) 975-5148
wjansen@nist.gov

NIST Cloud Computing Project

Cloud computing offers the possibility of increasing efficiency with a decrease in cost. However, as with any new technology, there are many questions about security. NIST is providing technical guidance and promoting standards promoting the effective and secure use of cloud computing within government and industry. Our first effort was to define cloud computing and its models. This guidance assists organizations in making informed decisions about procuring cloud services.

According to the NIST cloud computing definition, "cloud computing is a model for enabling convenient, on-demand network access to a shared pool of configurable computing resources (e.g., networks, servers, storage, applications, and services) that can be rapidly provisioned and released with minimal management effort or service provider interaction." The full extended definition describes five essential characteristics, three service models, and four deployment models. This definition is available from the CSD website (http://nist.gov/it/cloud/) and will be published in our upcoming NIST cloud computing Special Publication (SP).

The cloud computing team has formulated a strategy for facilitating the development of high-quality cloud computing standards. The strategy, Standards Acceleration to Jumpstart Adoption of Cloud Computing (SAJACC), describes a process for formulating cloud computing use cases and for judging the extent to which cloud system interfaces can satisfy them. An output of the SAJACC program will be test results about the sufficiency of selected cloud interfaces (or parts of their interfaces); these results will help standards development organizations to formulate their standards to achieve the central goals of portability, interoperability, and support for security. The SAJACC project will distribute results using a network-accessible portal that will also serve as a communication focal point between NIST and the larger technical community. As part of the SAJACC effort, the cloud computing team has developed an initial version of the SAJACC portal. The cloud computing project has also developed an initial set of twenty-four cloud system use cases, and has posted those use cases as working documents on the portal (http://www.nist.gov/itl/cloud/).

During FY2010, the cloud computing team also conducted a cloud computing forum at the Department of Commerce in May. There is a second forum planned for early FY2011, which will be held at NIST in early November. In addition, the cloud computing team is making progress on a SP on cloud computing that will be released as a public draft in the early part of FY2011.

The NIST cloud computing project is also supporting the cloud computing groups under the Federal CIO Council. This includes providing technical advice to the Cloud Computing Executive Steering Committee, the Cloud Computing Advisory Council, and the Information Security and Identity Management Committee's Web 2.0 working group.

http://www.nist.gov/itl/cloud/
Contact:
Mr. Lee Badger
(301) 975-3176
lee.badger@nist.gov

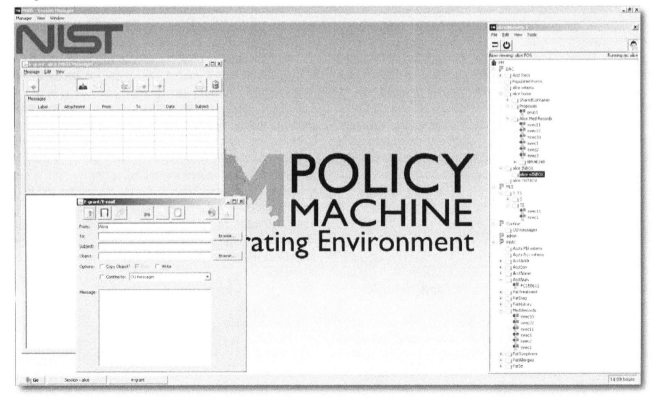

Policy Machine

The ability to control access to information in accordance with policy is perhaps the most fundamental security requirement. Unfortunately, despite over four decades of research, access control solutions remain inadequate for many practical applications.

We see two problems that contribute to, and if solved, could dramatically improve this situation. The first, referred to as the "policy enforcement problem", pertains to the limited ability for existing access control mechanisms to enforce a broad range of practical policies. While researchers, practitioners and policy makers have proposed a large variety of policy specifications and access control models to address real world security issues, only a relatively small subset of these policies can naturally (without extension) be enforced through off-the-shelf technology, and even fewer can be enforced by any one mechanism. Second is the "global policy enforcement problem": the difficulty or even inability to express and comprehensively enforce policies over objects that are stored, managed and processed in different environments. Through development of a standardized mechanism referred to as the "policy machine" (PM), NIST has taken an important step in addressing these two central problems:

- *Policy enforcement problem.* Can a policy unifying mechanism, one capable of expressing and enforcing the objectives of any policy, be devised? Although this is difficult to definitively answer given the open-endedness of "any policy", the policy machine identifies a small set of data relations, functions, and administrative operations that are reusable in the expression and enforcement of a wide variety of attribute-based policies.

- *Global policy enforcement problem.* Can a general operational environment enforce policy over arbitrary operation types on arbitrary (and meaningful) object types? Many IT operation and object types can be abstracted from a common set of access control primitives. A large variety of object types (e.g., files, email messages, and workflow work-items, records, fields, and clip boards) can be treated generically as PM objects and therefore controlled by the PM. This is because a large variety of operation types (read/write, send, approve, submit, insert, copy/cut/paste) can be implemented as PM recognized operations and/or as abstractions on that set of operations. Of further significance is that the PM not only enforces policy over operations on heterogeneous objects; it provides an environment where PM native features reduce or eliminate the need for application-level access control code.

To demonstrate the PM's viability, we developed and continue to revise a PM reference implementation capable of expressing and enforcing the objectives of diverse policies or combinations of policies, using a kernel simulator. We also demonstrated global policy enforcement over a rich set of applications and object types.

In FY2010, CSD, and other members of an Ad Hoc International Committee for Information Technology Standards working group began development of a three part PM standard under the title of "Next Generation Access Control" (NGAC). This work was conducted under three sub-projects:

- Project 2193-D: Next Generation Access Control –Implementation Requirements, Protocols and application programming interface (API) Definitions;

- Project 2194-D: Next Generation Access Control – Functional Architecture; and

- Project 2195-D: Next Generation Access Control - Generic Operations and Abstract Data Structures.

Also, in FY2010, NIST identified critical security requirements that will serve as the basis for selection of an architecture that will enable a robust PM deployment.

In the coming year we anticipate bringing all three parts of the NGAC proposed standard to ballot. In addition, in pursuit of a future open source release, we will select and implement the PM in an environment that meets the identified requirements with new and enhanced interfaces.

Contacts:
Mr. David Ferraiolo   Dr. Vincent Hu
(301) 975-3046   (301) 975-4975
david.ferraiolo@nist.gov   vhu@nist.gov

Security for Grid and Pervasive Systems

While grid and pervasive computing have become closer to reality in the last year, these technologies present challenges compared to static network systems with infrastructure security issues such as authorization, directory services, and firewalls. The research available on grid and pervasive security-related topics is generally targeted to a specific system, incomplete because of assumptions made, or ambiguous regarding the critical elements in their works. Because of the complexities of architecture and applications of the grid, a practical and conceptual guidance for their security is needed.

During FY2010, we continued our investigation on trust management frameworks, functional stacks, protocols, and application programming interfaces (APIs) for the pervasive systems' security functions, concentrating on those that have either been embedded or recommended by commercial or standards organizations. We also investigated the application of combining local and global access control policies in a virtual grid environment. Looking forward to FY2011, we expect that this project will:

- Promote (or accelerate) the adoption of community computing that utilizes the power of grid and pervasive infrastructure;

- Provide prototype security standards for the authorization management of community computing environments;

- Increase security and safety of static (connected) distributed systems by applying the trust domain concept of grid and pervasive computing; and

- Assist system architects, security administrators, and security managers whose expertise is related to community comput ing in managing their systems, and learning the limitations and practical approaches for their applications.

In FY2011, this project, Security for Grid and Pervasive Systems, will be merging with the Access Control and Privilege Management Research project.

Contact:
Dr. Vincent Hu
(301) 975-4975
vhu@nist.gov

Security Ontologies Modeling Quantitative Risk Analysis of Enterprise Systems

Over time, computer security has become a much diversified field of research. It has become increasingly difficult for experts of different domains to understand each other and to use a precisely defined terminology. Therefore, there is a need for a security ontology that can clearly define security related concepts and their relationships, and which can then be used to do quantitative risk analysis for enterprise information systems. The main goal of our research in this project is to develop an ontology that "knows" which threats endanger which assets and which countermeasures can reduce the probability of attacks. In addition each asset and each countermeasure in the ontology can be annotated with various types of cost as well as benefits. By comparing various scenarios during a quantitative risk analysis, companies can decide which safeguard options are more effective. The ontology will allow a shared and accurate knowledge of threats and countermeasures. It will provide objective data for decision making about which countermeasures to implement and a way to avoid implementation of countermeasures that are not cost effective.

In FY2010, we developed a security ontology that describes entities such as threats, vulnerabilities, countermeasures, assets and security objectives. We implemented this ontology using Protégé

and created a description of these entities in Resource Description Framework (RDF) and Web Ontology Language (OWL). In FY2011, we plan to develop graphical tools for a user to visualize and edit ontologies and to generate database schemas in Structured Query Language (SQL) that can be used to generate reports about enterprise level security metrics.

Contact:
Dr. Anoop Singhal
(301) 975-4432
anoop.singhal@nist.gov

Protecting Virtualization Technologies

Cloud Computing and Virtualization Laboratory

The objective of this work is to create a lab to evaluate the security of virtualization techniques and the cloud computing systems that employ them. The lab will serve as a resource for the development of ideas to mitigate security vulnerabilities in virtualized and cloud systems, and to gain hands-on experience that will inform NIST cloud and virtualizations guidelines. In FY2010, we conducted an initial study of the requirements of a lab that can support a wide variety of virtualization and cloud computing experiments, such as those involving multiple clouds or clouds comprised of diverse software. This resulted in the procurement of needed hardware and software resources as well as the necessary networking support to allow the lab's unimpeded access to the Internet.

In FY2011, CSD plans to deploy and test the hardware and software components of two primary setups to support a variety of virtualization solutions including both commercial and open source software such as VMWare vSphere, Citrix XenServer, and Microsoft Hyper-V hypervisors. CSD also plans to leverage the test environment to support some of the SAJACC use cases by implementing a proof of concept for supporting the NIST SP 800-53 security control requirements for low and moderate impact baseline in a cloud computing service model such as infrastructure as a service reference implementation.

Contact:
Mr. David Ferraiolo
(301) 975-3046
david.ferraiolo@nist.gov

Access Control and Identity Management in Virtualized Systems

The purpose of this project is to conduct research on how to integrate advanced access control mechanisms into virtualized systems. Access control has traditionally been integrated into either operating system mechanisms, network components (such as firewalls), or directly in applications. With a virtualized system, the option is available to add access control mechanisms into the hypervisor layer that implements the virtual machine abstractions. Such access control implementations may leverage the isolation feature offered by virtualized systems. This research analyzes the requirements for adding access control at the different layers, and the impact on different access control components such as users, processes, policy enforcements points, policy decision points, and policy database coordinated.

George Mason University (GMU) has developed a method for creating lightweight virtualized environments that act as application wrappers, providing: the ability to track application interactions; process isolation; and, the ability to intercept process requests for accessing system resources. In FY2010, CSD collaborated with GMU to begin to integrate and extend a NIST developed access control framework into their virtualization framework. This collaboration presents the opportunity to extend NIST's framework beyond file system resources to control over network and application communications.

Contact:
Mr. David Ferraiolo
(301) 975-3046
david.ferraiolo@nist.gov

Automated Vulnerability Management

Security Content Automation Protocol (SCAP)

To support the overarching security automation vision, it is necessary to have both trusted information and a standardized means to store and share it. Through close work with its government and industry partners, NIST has developed the Security Content Automation Protocol (SCAP) to provide the standardized technical mechanisms to share information between systems. Through the National Vulnerability Database (NVD) and the National Checklist Program (NCP), NIST is providing relevant and important information in the areas of vulnerability and configuration management. Combined, SCAP and the programs that leverage it are moving the information assurance industry towards being able to standardize communications, collect and store relevant data in standardized formats, and provide automated means for the assessment and remediation of systems for both vulnerabilities and configuration compliance.

SCAP is a suite of specifications that use eXtensible Markup Language (XML) to standardize the format and nomenclature by which security software products communicate information about software flaws and security configurations. SCAP includes software flaw and security configuration standard reference data, also known as SCAP content. This reference data is provided by the NVD (http://nvd.nist.gov/), which is managed by NIST and sponsored by the Department of Homeland Security (DHS).

SCAP is a multi-purpose protocol that supports automated vulnerability checking, technical control compliance activities, and security measurement. The U.S. Government, in cooperation with academia and private industry, is adopting SCAP and encourages its use in support of security automation activities and initiatives.

Draft NIST SP 800-126 Revision 1, *The Technical Specification for the Security Content Automation Protocol (SCAP): SCAP Version 1.1*; is the SCAP technical specification (http://csrc.nist.gov/publications/drafts/800-126-r1/second-public-draft_sp800-126r1-may2010.pdf). CSD plans to publish SP 800-126 Revision 1 in final form in the first quarter of FY2011. This document describes the seven component specifications comprising SCAP:

- Extensible Configuration Checklist Description Format (XCCDF), an XML specification for structured collections of security configuration rules used by operating system and application platforms;

- Open Vulnerability and Assessment Language (OVAL), an XML specification for exchanging technical details on how to check systems for security-related software flaws, configuration issues, and patches;

- Open Checklist Interactive Language (OCIL), an XML specification for expressing questionnaires to collect information that requires interacting with people, such as asking them about training they have participated in, and also to harvest information stored during an organization's previous data collection efforts, such as audits;

- Common Configuration Enumeration (CCE), a dictionary of names for software security configuration issues (e.g., access control settings, password policy settings);

- Common Platform Enumeration (CPE), a naming convention for hardware, operating systems, and application products;

- Common Vulnerabilities and Exposures (CVE), a dictionary of names for publicly known security-related software flaws; and

- Common Vulnerability Scoring System (CVSS), a method for classifying characteristics of software flaws and assigning severity scores based on these characteristics.

SCAP is being widely adopted by major software and hardware manufacturers and has become a significant component of information security management and governance programs. The protocol is expected to evolve and expand in support of the growing need to define and measure effective security controls, assess and monitor ongoing aspects of information security, remediate non-compliance, and successfully manage systems in accordance with the Risk Management Framework described in NIST SP 800-

53, *Recommended Security Controls for Federal Information Systems and Organizations* (The Risk Management Framework is described within SP 800-53, available at http://csrc.nist.gov/publications/.)

Currently, CSD is leveraging SCAP in multiple areas, both to support our own mission and to enable other agencies and private sector entities to meet their goals. For CSD, SCAP is a critical component of the SCAP Validation Program, the NVD, and the National Checklist Program.

Contact:
Mr. Dave Waltermire
(301) 975-3390
david.waltermire@nist.gov

National Vulnerability Database (NVD)

The National Vulnerability Database (NVD) is the U.S. Government repository of standards-based vulnerability management reference data. The NVD provides information regarding security vulnerabilities and configuration settings, vulnerability impact metrics, technical assessment methods, and references to remediation assistance and IT product identification data. The NVD reference data supports security automation efforts based on the Security Content Automation Protocol (SCAP). As of October 2010, NVD contained the following resources:

- Over 45,000 vulnerability advisories with an average of 13 new vulnerabilities added daily;

- 23 SCAP-expressed checklists containing thousands of low-level security configuration checks that can be used by SCAP validated security products to perform automated evaluations of system state;

- 142 non-SCAP security checklists (e.g., English prose guidance and configuration scripts);

- 212 U.S. Computer Emergency Readiness Team (US-CERT) alerts, 2,473 US-CERT vulnerability summaries, and 6,057 SCAP machine-readable software flaw checks;

- Product dictionary with 30,441 operating system, application, and hardware name entries; and

- 28,051 vulnerability advisories translated into Spanish.

NVD is sponsored by the Department of Homeland Security's National Cyber Security Division.

NVD's effective reach has been extended by the use of NVD SCAP data by commercial security products deployed in thousands of organizations worldwide. Increased adoption of SCAP is evidenced by the increasing demand for NVD XML data feeds and SCAP-expressed content from the NVD website. Concerted outreach efforts over the last year have resulted in an increase in the number of vendors providing SCAP-expressed content.

NVD continues to play a pivotal role in the Payment Card Industry (PCI) efforts to mitigate vulnerabilities in credit card systems. PCI mandates the use of NVD vulnerability severity scores in measuring the risk to payment card servers worldwide and for prioritizing vulnerability patching. PCI's use of NVD severity scores helps enhance credit card transaction security and protects consumers' personal information.

Throughout FY2010, NVD continued to provide access to vulnerability reference data and security checklists. NVD deployed an enhanced checklist submission web interface and a web service checklist submission capability is nearing completion. Additionally, the NVD now hosts an SCAP Content Validation Tool that can be used by creators of SCAP content to ensure that their SCAP content packages conform to NIST SP 800-126, The Technical Specification for the Security Content Automation Protocol (SCAP): SCAP Version 1.0; guidelines. Finally, NVD now supports automated SCAP content generation from the Common Vulnerabilities and Exposures (CVE) vulnerability data feed. NVD data is a fundamental component of our security automation infrastructure and is substantially increasing the security of networks worldwide. CSD plans to expand and improve the NVD in FY2011.

---

http://nvd.nist.gov
Contacts:
Mr. John Banghart   Mr. Harold Booth
(301) 975-8514   (301) 975-8441
john.banghart@nist.gov   harold.booth@nist.gov

National Checklist Program

There are many threats to information technology (IT), ranging from remotely launched network service exploits to malicious code spread through infected e-mails, websites, and downloaded files. Vulnerabilities in IT products are discovered daily, and many ready-to-use exploitation techniques are widely available on the Internet. Because IT products are often intended for a wide variety of audiences, restrictive security configuration controls are usually not enabled by default. As a result, many out-of-the-box IT products are immediately vulnerable. In addition, identifying a reasonable set of security settings that achieve balanced risk management is a complicated, arduous, and time-consuming task, even for experienced system administrators.

To facilitate development of security configuration checklists for IT products and to make checklists more organized and usable, NIST established the National Checklist Program (NCP) in furtherance of its statutory responsibilities under the Federal Information Security Management Act (FISMA) of 2002, Public Law 107-347, and also under the Cyber Security Act, which tasks NIST to "develop, and revise as necessary, a checklist setting forth settings and option selections that minimize the security risks associated with each computer hardware or software system that is, or is likely to become widely used within the Federal Government." In February 2008, revised Part 39 of the Federal Acquisition Regulation (FAR) was published. Paragraph (d) of section 39.101 states, "In acquiring information technology, agencies shall include the appropriate IT security policies and requirements, including use of common security configurations available from the NIST website at : http://checklists.nist.gov. Agency contracting officers should consult with the requiring official to ensure the appropriate standards are incorporated." In Memorandum M08-22, Office of Management and Budget (OMB) mandated the use of SCAP Validated products for continuous monitoring of Federal Desktop Core Configuration (FDCC) compliance. The NCP strives to encourage and make simple agencies' compliance with these mandates.

The goals of the NCP are to:

- Facilitate development and sharing of checklists by providing a formal framework for checklist developers to submit checklists to NIST;

- Provide guidance to developers to help them create standardized, high-quality checklists that conform to common operations environments;

- Help developers and users by providing guidelines for making checklists better documented and more usable;

- Encourage software vendors and other parties to develop checklists;

- Provide a managed process for the review, update, and maintenance of checklists;

- Provide an easy-to-use repository of checklists; and

- Encourage the use of automation technologies for checklist application such as SCAP.

There are 162 checklists posted on the website; 24 of the checklists are SCAP-expressed (see section on SCAP above) and can be used with SCAP-validated products. It is anticipated that a minimum of several more SCAP-expressed checklists will be added in FY2011 as contributions come from other federal agencies and product vendors. Organizations can use checklists obtained from the NCP website (http://checklists.nist.gov) for automated security configuration patch assessment. NCP currently hosts SCAP checklists for Internet Explorer 7.0, Internet Explorer 8.0, Office 2007, Red Hat Enterprise Linux, Windows 7, Windows Vista, Windows XP and other

products.

To assist users in identifying automated checklist content, NCP groups checklists into tiers, from Tier I to Tier IV. NCP uses the tiers to rank checklists according to their automation capability. Tier III and IV checklists are considered production-ready and have been validated by the SCAP content validation tool as conforming to the requirements outlined in NIST SP 800-126, The Technical Specification for the Security Content Automation Protocol (SCAP). Tier IV checklists are used in the SCAP validation program (see following section for details) when validating SCAP products. Tier III checklists are not presently used in the SCAP validation program; however, Tier III checklists should be compatible with SCAP-validated products. Tier II checklists document recommended security settings in a machine-readable, non-standard format, such as a proprietary format or a product-specific configuration script. Tier I checklists are prose-based and contain no machine-readable content. Users can browse the checklists based on the checklist tier, IT product, IT product category, or authority, and also through a keyword search that searches the checklist name and summary for user-specified terms. The search results show the detailed checklist metadata and a link to any SCAP content for the checklist, as well as links to any supporting resources associated with the checklist.

The NCP is defined in NIST SP 800-70 Revision 2, *National Checklist Program for IT Products—Guidelines for Checklist Users and Developers*, which can be found at http://csrc.nist.gov/publications/.

---

http://checklists.nist.gov
Contact:
Mr. Stephen Quinn
(301) 975-6967
stephen.quinn@nist.gov

Security Content Automation Protocol (SCAP) Validation Program

The SCAP Validation Program performs conformance testing to ensure that products correctly implement SCAP as defined in NIST SP 800-126. Conformance testing is necessary because SCAP is a complex specification consisting of six individual specifications that work together to meet various use cases. A single error in product implementation could result in undetected vulnerabilities or policy non-compliance within agency and industry networks.

The SCAP Validation Program was created by request of the Office of Management and Budget to support the Federal Desktop Core Configuration (FDCC). The Program coordinates its work with the NIST National Voluntary Laboratory Accreditation Program (NVLAP) to set up independent conformance testing laboratories that conduct the testing based on draft NISTIR 7511 Revision 2, *Security Content Automation Protocol (SCAP) Version 1.0 Validation Program Test Requirements*. When testing is completed, the laboratory submits a test report to CSD for review and approval. SCAP validation testing has been designed to be inexpensive, yet effective. The SCAP conformance tests are either easily human verifiable or automated through NIST provided reference tools. To date, the program has accredited ten independent laboratories and validated 40 products from 30 different vendors.

While FDCC SCAP testing is an important part of the program, it is only one of several SCAP capabilities which vendors can apply to test their products. The others cover product capabilities such as configuration scanning, vulnerability scanning, patch checking, and remediation capabilities.

The SCAP Validation Program will expand in FY2011 to include additional capabilities, provide enhanced testing support, and evolve to include new technologies as SCAP itself matures. Current expansion includes support for the U.S. Government Configuration Baseline initiative, which plans to release configuration baselines for Microsoft Windows 7/IE8 and Red Hat Enterprise Linux 5.

---

http://scap.nist.gov/validation/
Contact:
Mr. John Banghart
(301) 975-8514
john.banghart@nist.gov

Technical Security Metrics

Measurement is the key to making major advancements in any scientific field, and computer security is no exception. Measures give us a standardized way of expressing and quantifying security characteristics. Because of the ever-increasing complexity of threats, vulnerabilities, and mitigation strategies, there is a particularly strong need for additional research on attack, vulnerability, and security control measurements. Improved measurement capabilities in these areas would allow organizations to make scientifically sound decisions when planning, implementing, and configuring security controls. This would improve the effectiveness of security controls, while reducing cost by eliminating unnecessary and ineffective controls.

In FY2010, CSD continued its long-term research efforts on technical security metrics. The first stage of this work, which is nearing completion, involves developing specifications for measuring and scoring individual vulnerabilities, and researching how vulnerabilities from multiple hosts can be used in sequence to compromise particular targets. A summary of these efforts from the past year is presented below.

Vulnerability Measurement and Scoring

The Common Vulnerability Scoring System (CVSS) is an industry standard that enables the security community to calculate the relative severity of software flaw vulnerabilities within information technology systems through sets of security metrics and formulas. During the past year, NIST security staff continued to provide technical leadership in determining how CVSS could be adapted for use with other types of vulnerabilities besides software flaws. This work has involved evaluating and refining the following draft specifications:

- The Common Misuse Scoring System (CMSS), which was originally proposed in draft NISTIR 7517, *The Common Misuse Scoring System (CMSS): Metrics for Software Feature Misuse Vulnerabilities*. CMSS adapts CVSS for use with software feature misuse and trust relationship abuse vulnerabilities.

- The Common Configuration Scoring System (CCSS), which was originally proposed in draft NISTIR 7502, *The Common Configuration Scoring System (CCSS): Metrics for Software Security Configuration Vulnerabilities*. CCSS is based on CVSS and CMSS but has been customized for use with software security configuration-related vulnerabilities.

During the first half of FY2011, we plan on finalizing the CMSS and CCSS specifications. This will complete the first stage of CSD's technical security metrics research. The second stage of the work is expected to involve supporting the implementation of these specifications, such as creating standardized reference data for CCSS, and researching how all three specifications—CVSS, CCSS, and CMSS—can be used together to better conceptualize and quantify the security posture of systems.

Contact:
John Banghart
(301) 975-8514
john.banghart@nist.gov

Network Security Analysis Using Attack Graphs

The objective of this research is to develop a standard model for measuring security of computer networks. A standard model will enable us to answer questions such as "Are we more secure now than yesterday?", or "How does the security of one network configuration compare with another one?" Also, having a standard model to measure network security will allow users, vendors and researchers to evaluate methodologies and products for network security in a coherent and consistent manner.

Good metrics should be able to be measured consistently, be inexpensive to collect, be expressed numerically, have units of measure, and have specific context. CSD has approached the challenge of network security analysis by capturing vulnerability interdependencies and measuring security in the exact way that real attackers penetrate the network. Our methodology for security risk analysis is based on the model of attack graphs. We analyze all attack paths through a network, providing a probabilistic metric of the overall system risk. Through this metric, we analyze trade-offs between security costs and security benefits. Our metric is consistent, unambiguous, and provides context for understanding security risk of computer networks.

In FY2010, we developed a new model of security analysis for "zero day" attacks. We proposed a novel security metric called k zero day safety, based on the number of unknown zero day vulnerabilities. The metric counts how many unknown vulnerabilities would be required to compromise a network asset. We also did performance analysis of our techniques to understand how our method will scale up for enterprise networks consisting of multiple hosts.

In FY2011, we plan to integrate the proposed techniques into existing attack graph-based security tools and validate our results. We also plan to publish our results in conferences and journals.

Contact:
Dr. Anoop Singhal
(301) 975-4432
anoop.singhal@nist.gov

Infrastructure Services, Protocols, and Applications

Internet Protocol Version 6 (IPv6) and Internet Protocol Security (IPsec)

Internet Protocol Version 6 (IPv6) is an updated version of the current Internet Protocol, IPv4. The primary motivations for the development of IPv6 were to increase the number of unique IP addresses and to handle the needs of new Internet applications and devices. In addition, IPv6 was designed with the following goals: increased ease of network management and configuration, expandable IP headers, improved mobility and security, and quality of service controls. IPv6 has been, and continues to be, developed and defined by the Internet Engineering Task Force (IETF).

This year, the NIST IPv6 Test Program became operational. The goal of this program is to provide assurance on IPv6 conformance and interoperability of products. Three test labs were accredited for testing, and a Supplier's Declaration of Conformity (SDOC) template was published to enable vendors of IPv6 products to report the details of their products that have successfully executed the United States Government IPv6 (USGv6) tests which are detailed for both vendors and accreditors in two documents: SP 500-273, *USGv6 Test Methods: General Description and Validation - Version 2.0* and SP 500-281, *USGv6 Testing Program User's Guide*. These documents and the SDOC template can be found at: http://www.antd.nist.gov/usgv6/testing.html.

In September 2010, OMB issued a Memorandum[7] requiring government agencies to meet additional IPv6-related goals. The

memo states: "To facilitate the federal government's adoption of IPv6, OMB will work with NIST to continue the evolution and implementation of the USGv6 Profile and Testing Program. This Program will provide the technical basis for expressing requirements for IPv6 technologies and will test commercial products' support of corresponding capabilities."

A draft of SP 800-119, *Guidelines for the Secure Deployment of IPv6,* was posted for public comment in FY2010. This document describes and analyzes the numerous protocols that comprise IPv6, including addressing, domain name system (DNS), routing, mobility, quality of service, multihoming, IPsec, etc. For each component, there is a detailed analysis of the differences between IPv4 and IPv6, the security ramifications and any unknown aspects. New sections were added to address late-breaking, significant changes in the approach to IPv6 transition. The final version will be published in FY2011.

In FY2011, NIST will continue to manage and evolve the USGv6 Test Program; the NIST IPv6 Profile will also be updated.

Contacts:
Ms. Sheila Frankel   Mr. Douglas Montgomery (ANTD)
(301) 975-3297   (301) 975-3630
sheila.frankel@nist.gov   dougm@nist.gov

Securing the Domain Name System (DNS)

The Domain Name System (DNS) is a global distributed system in which Internet addresses in mnemonic form such as http://csrc.nist.gov are converted into the equivalent numeric Internet Protocol (IP) addresses such as 129.6.13.39. Certain servers throughout the world maintain the databases needed, as well as perform the translations. A DNS server that is performing a translation may communicate with other Internet DNS servers if it does not have the data needed to translate the address itself.

As with other Internet-based systems, DNS is subject to several threats. To counter these threats, the Internet Engineering Task Force (IETF) developed a set of specifications for securing DNS called DNS Security Extensions (DNSSEC) to provide origin authentication and data integrity for all responses from the DNS. In partnership with the Department of Homeland Security, NIST has been actively involved in promoting the deployment of DNSSEC since 2004.

---

[7]. http://www.cio.gov/documents/IPv6MemoFINAL.pdf

The significant achievements in FY2010 are as follows:

- Publication of the revised version of SP 800-81 Revision 1, *Secure Domain Name System (DNS) Deployment Guide*, in April 2010, after two rounds of public comments. The major additions/changes in this revision are the following:

  o Updated recommendations for all cryptographic operations relating to digital signing of DNS records, verification of the signatures, Zone Transfer, Dynamic Updates, Key Management and Authenticated Denial of Existence;

  o The addition of IETF RFC documents that have formed the basis for the updated recommendations including: DNNSEC Operational Practices (RFC 4641), Automated Updates for DNS Security (DNSSEC) Trust Anchors (RFC 5011), DNS Security (DNSSEC) Hashed Authenticated Denial of Existence (RFC 5155) and HMAC SHA TSIG Algorithm Identifiers (RFC 4635).

  o Additional FIPS standards and NIST guidelines incorporated into the updated recommendations including: FIPS 198-1, *Keyed-Hash Message Authentication Code (HMAC)*, FIPS 186-3, *Digital Signature Standard,* and SP 800-57 Part 1 and Part 3, *Recommendations for Key Management;*

  o Illustration of secure configuration examples using DNS Software offering NSD, in addition to Berkeley Internet Name Domain (BIND);

  o Guidelines on procedures for migrating to a new Cryptographic Algorithm for signing of the Zone (Section 11.5);

  o Guidelines for procedures for migrating to Next Secure 3 (NSEC3) specifications from NSEC for providing authenticated denial of existence (Section 11.6);

  o Deployment Guidelines for Split-Zone under different scenarios (Section 11.7).

- Assisting GSA in deploying DNSSEC on the .gov Top Level Domain (TLD), to meet the OMB mandate. NIST provided a technical review of contractor plans, and developed a comprehensive test plan for the .gov delegation holder interface on http://www.dotgov.gov/. The DNSSEC deployment was successful, with NIST continuing to provide technical support for contractors.

- Assisting the National Telecommunications and Information Administration (NTIA) in successfully deploying DNSSEC at the root "." Zone in July 2010. This was one of the major events in the Internet Infrastructure in the past decade. NIST played a key in developing the initial requirements, as well as providing technical review for all documents produced by NTIA and their contractors.

- Continuing the Secure Naming Infrastructure Pilot (SNIP) operations in 2010. The SNIP is a distributed test bed to help U.S. government DNS administrators deploy DNSSEC and test new DNSSEC implementations.

- Hosting a session in FOSE 2010 consisting of presentations and question and answer sessions for assisting agencies with DNSSEC deployments.

Contacts:

Dr. Ramaswamy Chandramouli
(301) 975-5013
mouli@nist.gov

Mr. Scott Rose
(ANTD)
(301) 975-8439
scott.rose@nist.gov

CSD's Part in National and International IT Security Standards Processes

Figure 1 (next page) below shows the many national and international standards developing organizations (SDO's) involved in cybersecurity standardization.

The International Organization for Standardization

The International Organization for Standardization (ISO) is a network of the national standards institutes of 148 countries, with the representation of one member per country. The scope of ISO covers standardization in all fields except electrical and electronic engineering standards, which are the responsibility of the International Electrotechnical Commission (IEC).

The IEC prepares and publishes international standards for all electrical, electronic, and related technologies, including electronics, magnetics and electromagnetics, electroacoustics, multimedia, telecommunication, and energy production and distribution, as well as associated general disciplines such as terminology and symbols, electromagnetic compatibility, measurement and performance, dependability, design and development, safety, and the environment.

Joint Technical Committee 1 (JTC1) was formed by ISO and IEC to be responsible for international standardization in the field of Information Technology. It develops, maintains, promotes, and facilitates IT standards required by global markets meeting business and user requirements concerning—

- Design and development of IT systems and tools;

- Performance and quality of IT products and systems;

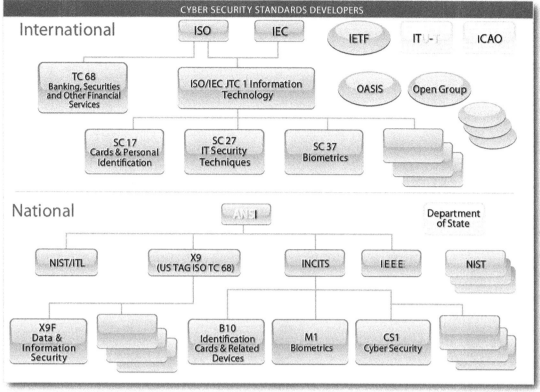

(Figure 1)

- Security of IT systems and information;

- Portability of application programs;

- Interoperability of IT products and systems;

- Unified tools and environments;

- Harmonized IT vocabulary; and

- User-friendly and ergonomically designed user interfaces.

JTC1 consists of a number of subcommittees (SCs) and working groups that address specific technologies. SCs that produce standards relating to IT security include:

- SC 06 - Telecommunications and Information Exchange Between Systems;

- SC 17 - Cards and Personal Identification;

- SC 27 - IT Security Techniques; and

- SC 37 – Biometrics (Fernando Podio of NIST serves as Chair).

JTC1 also has—

- Technical Committee 68 – Financial Services;

- SC 2 - Operations and Procedures including Security;

- SC 4 – Securities;

- SC 6 - Financial Transaction Cards, Related Media and Operations; and

- SC 7 - Core Banking.

The American National Standards Institute

The American National Standards Institute (ANSI) is a private, non-profit organization (501(c)(3)) that administers and coordinates the United States voluntary standardization and conformity assessment system.

ANSI facilitates the development of American National Standards (ANSs) by accrediting the procedures of standards-developing organizations (SDOs). The InterNational Committee for Information Technology Standards (INCITS) is accredited by ANSI.

ANSI promotes the use of U.S. standards internationally, advocates U.S. policy and technical positions in international and regional standards organizations, and encourages the adoption of international standards as national standards where they meet the needs of the user community.

ANSI is the sole U.S. representative and dues-paying member of the two major non-treaty international standards organizations,

ISO and, via the United States National Committee (USNC), the IEC.

INCITS serves as the ANSI Technical Advisory Group (TAG) for ISO/IEC Joint Technical Committee 1. INCITS is sponsored by the Information Technology Industry (ITI) Council, a trade association representing the leading United States providers of information technology products and services. INCITS currently has more than 800 published standards.

INCITS is organized into Technical Committees that focus on the creation of standards for different technology areas. Technical committees that focus on IT security and IT security-related technologies, or may require separate security standards include:

- B10 – Identification Cards and Related Devices;

- CS1 – Cyber Security;

- E22 – Item Authentication;

- M1 – Biometrics;

- T3 – Open Distributed Processing (ODP);

- T6 – Radio Frequency Identification (RFID) Technology;

- Corporate Governance of IT (CGIT1); and

- Distributed Application Platforms and Services (DAPS38).

As a technical committee of INCITS, CS1 develops United States, national, ANSI-accredited standards in the area of cyber security. Its scope encompasses—

- Management of information security and systems;

- Management of third-party information security service providers;

- Intrusion detection;

- Network security;

- Incident handling;

- IT security evaluation and assurance;

- Security assessment of operational systems;

- Security requirements for cryptographic modules;

- Protection profiles;

- Role-based access control;

- Security checklists;

- Security metrics;

- Cryptographic and non-cryptographic techniques and mechanisms including:

    o confidentiality,

    o entity authentication,

    o non-repudiation,

    o key management,

    o data integrity,
    o message authentication,

    o hash functions, and

    o digital signatures;

- Future service and applications standards supporting the implementation of control objectives and controls as defined in ISO 27001, in the areas of—

    o business continuity, and

    o outsourcing;

- Identity management, including:

    o identity management framework,

    o role-based access control, and

    o single sign-on;

- Privacy technologies, including:

    o privacy framework,

    o privacy reference architecture,

    o privacy infrastructure,

    o anonymity and credentials, and

    o specific privacy enhancing technologies.

The scope of CS1 explicitly excludes the areas of work on cyber security standardization presently underway in INCITS B10, M1, T3, T10 and T11; as well as other standard groups, such as the Alliance for Telecommunications Industry Solutions, the Institute of Electrical and Electronics Engineers, Inc., the Internet Engineering Task Force, the Travel Industry Association of America, and Accredited Standards Committee (ASC) X9. The CS1 scope of work includes standardization in most of the same cyber security areas as are covered in the NIST Computer Security Division.

As the U.S. TAG to ISO/IEC JTC 1/SC 27, CS1 contributes to the SC 27 program of work on IT Security Techniques in terms of comments and contributions on SC 27 standards projects; votes on SC 27 standards documents at various stages of development; and identifies U.S. experts to work on various SC 27 projects or to serve in various SC 27 leadership positions. Currently a number of CS1 members are serving as SC 27 document editors or coeditors on various standards projects, including Randy Easter of NIST for ISO/IEC 24759, *Test Requirements for Cryptographic Modules* and the revision of ISO/IEC 19790 *Security requirements for cryptographic modules,* and Allen Roginsky of NIST, Co-Editor on 29150, *Signcryption.* Erika McCallister recently took over as Editor of 29115, *Entity authentication assurance.* Richard Kissel has recently been nominated as a Co-Editor for the revision of ISO/IEC 27000 – *Information security management systems – Overview and vocabulary.*

All input from CS1 goes through INCITS to ANSI, then to SC 27. It is also a conduit for getting U.S.-based new work item proposals and U.S.-developed national standards into the international SC 27 standards development process. In its international efforts, CS1 has consistently, efficiently, and in a timely manner responded to all calls for contributions on all international security standards projects in ISO/IEC JTC1 SC 27. In addition CS1 is making contributions on several new areas of work in SC 27, including:

- ISO/IEC 27038 – Specification for digital redaction (WG 4);

- ISO/IEC 29192-1 – Light-weight cryptography – Part 1: General (WG 2);

- ISO/IEC 29192-2 – Light-weight cryptography – Part 2: Block ciphers (WG 2);

- ISO/IEC 29192-3 – Light-weight cryptography – Part 3: Stream ciphers (WG 2);

- ISO/IEC 29192-4 – Light-weight cryptography – Part 4: Mechanisms using asymmetric techniques (WG 2);

- ISO/IEC 20008-1 -- Anonymous digital signatures – Part 1: General (WG 2);

- ISO/IEC 20008-2 -- Anonymous digital signatures – Part 2: Mechanisms using a group public key (WG 2);

- ISO/IEC 20009-1 -- Anonymous entity authentication – Part 1: General (WG 2);

- ISO/IEC 20009-2 -- Anonymous entity authentication – Part 2: Mechanisms based on anonymous digital signature schemes (WG 2);

- ISO/IEC 29193 – Secure system engineering principles and techniques ; and

- ISO/IEC 20004 -- Software development and evaluation under ISO/IEC 15408 (WG 3).

Through its membership on CS1, where Dan Benigni serves as the nonvoting chair, and Richard Kissel is the NIST Primary with voting privileges, NIST contributes to all CS1 national and international IT security standards efforts. Internationally, there are over 80 published standards, and almost all are National Standards. There are more than 63 current international standards projects.

CSD's Role in Cybersecurity Standardization

CSD's cybersecurity research plays a direct role in the Cybersecurity Standardization efforts of CS1. During this fiscal year:

1) The CS1 Task Group CS1.1 Role-Based Access Control (RBAC) has finished and INCITS is about to publish the national standard titled "*Requirements for the Implementation and Interoperability of Role Based Access Control*". In addition, the task group has started work on the revision of INCITS 359 – 2004, "Role Based Access Control (RBAC)", as well as INCITS Project: 2215-D, "Information technology -- Role Based Access Control – Policy Enhanced" and Project 2214-D, "Process for Defining Roles for Role Based Access Control." NIST originally authored RBAC, and both Rick Kuhn and Richard Kissel are working in this task group.

2) The NIST Policy Machine research and development has resulted in three national projects that CS1 has recommended, and for which the INCITS Executive Board has approved as national standards projects:

a) Next Generation Access Control-Implementation Requirements, Protocols and API Definitions (NGAC-IRPADS). It is assigned project number is 2193-D, and Roger Cummings of Smantec is the editor;

b) Next Generation Access Control – Functional Architecture (NGAC-FA). It is assigned project number is 2194-D, and David Ferraiolo of NIST is the editor; and

c) Next Generation Access Control - Generic Operations & Abstract Data Structures (NGAC-GOADS)). It is assigned project number is 2195-D, and Serban Gavrila of NIST is the editor.

3) CS1 has an ad hoc group working on the national standards project titled *"Small Organization Baseline Information Security Handbook"*. The NIST Principal member of CS1 is Richard Kissel, whose job is to speak to small business on security. NISTIR 7621, *Small Business Information Security: The Fundamentals*, is the base document for this CS1 national standards project. This work will have a direct impact on CSD's outreach on security to small and medium sized businesses in future.

Within CS1, liaisons are maintained with nearly 20 organizations. They include the following:

- Open Group;

- IEEE P1700;

- Forum of Incident Response and Security Teams (FIRST);

- IEEE P1619;

- American Bar Association (ABA), section on Science and Technology;

- INCITS T11;

- INCITS M1;

- Financial Services Technology Consortium (FSTC);

- Internet Security Alliance;

- Kantara Initiative Identity Assurance Working Group (IAWG);

- INCITS PL 22;

- SC 7 TAG;

- Commercial Data Privacy Coordinating Committee (CDPCC);

- INCITS Technical Committee on Corporate Governance of IT;

- Scientific Working Group on Digital Evidence (SWGDE);

- ITU-T Q4/17 ;

- ITU-T Q10/17 ;

- Software Assurance Forum for Excellence in Code (SAFECode);

Contact:
Mr. Daniel Benigni
(301) 975-3279
benigni@nist.gov

Systems and Emerging Technologies Security Research (SETS) Group Guidelines and Documents

SETS's guidelines and documents along with the abstracts to these documents can be found in the Publications section on page 51-60.

Honors And Awards

Department of Commerce - Gold Medal Award:

Kelley Dempsey, Peggy Himes, Arnold Johnson, Ron Ross, Marianne Swanson, Patricia Toth

The group is recognized for its interagency leadership and technical excellence in creating the Risk Management Framework, a methodology for incorporating sound security risk management practices throughout the information system life cycle. This work, performed in support of FISMA, has been adopted government wide to improve the security of government systems and information. The impact of the work includes preventing compromises of government systems and information, increasing confidence in sharing data and services among agencies, and lowering security operational costs.

Front (Left to Right): Kelley Dempsey, Marianne Swanson,
Back (L to R): Ron Ross, Peggy Himes, and Arnold Johnson
Not Pictured: Patricia Toth

Federal 100 Award:

Dr. Ron Ross is responsible for leading NIST's Federal Information Security Management Act Implementation Project through the development of standards and guidelines.

Dr. Ron Ross
Senior Computer Scietnist

He also is the project leader, creator and primary author of NIST's Risk Management Framework and has overseen development of a library of supporting technical standards and guidelines published in the Federal Information Processing Standards and 800 series of special publications. The framework fundamentally changed the way agencies protect information systems, enabling them to significantly reduce vulnerabilities.

"Ross has provided extraordinary research and technical leadership in the field of information security and the unification of information security concept and practices in the federal government," said Matthew Scholl, manager of NIST's Security Management and Assurance Group.

Annabelle Lee Received the Smart Grid Interoperability Panel (SGIP) certificate of appreciation for 2010

Pictured Left to Right:
Steve Widergren, Smart Grid Interoperability Panel Chair, Pacific Northwest National Laboratory; Annabelle Lee, NIST; Dr. George Arnold, National Coordinator for Smart Grid Standards, NIST; Mark Klerer, Smart Grid Interoperability Panel Vice Chair, Qualcomm

Launching the Cybersecurity Coordinating Task Group (CSCTG), Ms. Lee had only a notion of what was expected, which was simply to identify ways to make the grid secure. Organizing an army of several hundred volunteers, she quickly identified workgroups and a structure to support the task of generating and delivering the NIST Interagency Report 7628 (NISTIR) that has become the baseline for all future security efforts for the entire Smart Grid community in the United States.

Key to Publications:
FIPS – Federal Information Processing Standards
SP – Special Publications
NISTIR – NIST Interagency Report

Draft Publications

Type & Number	Title	Date Released	Finalized in FY2010
FIPS-140-3	Revised DRAFT Security Requirements for Cryptographic Modules	December 2009	No
SP 800-135	Recommendation for Existing Application-Specific Key Derivation Functions	August 2010	No
SP 800-132	Recommendation for Passwod-Based Key Derivation - Part 1: Storage Applications	June 2010	No
SP 800-131	Recommendation for the Trainsitioning of Cryptographic Algorithms and Key Sizes	2 Drafts released: January and June 2010	No
SP 800-130	A Framework for Designing Crptyographic Key Management Systems	June 2010	No
SP 800-128	Guide for Security Configuration Management of Information Systems	March 2010	No
SP 800-126 Revision 1	The Technical Specification for the Secuirty Content Automation Protocol (SCAP): SCAP Version 1.1	2 Drafts released: Decemeber 2009 and May 2010	Yes - Nov. 2009
SP 800-125	Guide to Secuirty for Full Virtualization Technologies	July 2010	No
SP 800-119	Guidelines for the Secure Deployment of IPv6	February 2010	No
SP 800-85A-2	PIV Card Application and Middleware Interface Test Guidelines (SP8000-73-3 compliance)	May 2010	Yes - July 2010
SP 800-78-2	Crytographic Algorithms and Key Sizes for Personal Identifcation Verification (PIV)	October 2009	Yes - Feb. 2010
SP 800-56C	Recommendation for Key Derivation Through Extraction-then-Expansion	September 2010	No
SP 800-53A Revision 1	Guide for Assessing the Security Controls in Deferal Information Systems and Organizations	May 2010	Yes - June 2010
Draft Addendum to SP 800-38A	Recommendation for Block Cipher Modes of Operation: Three Variants of Ciphertext Stealing for CBC Mode	July 2010	No
SP 800-37 Revision 1	Guide for Applying the Risk Management Framework to Federal Information Systems: A Security Life Cycle Approach	November 2010	Yes - Feb. 2010
SP 800-34 Revision 1	Contingency Planning Guide for Federal Information Systems	October 2009	Yes - May 2010
NISTIR 7697	Common Platform Enumeration: Dictionary Specification Version 2.3	August 2010	No
NISTIR 7696	Common Platform Enumeration: Name Matching Specification Version 2.3	August 2010	No
NISTIR 7695	Common Platform Enumeration: Naming Specification Version 2.3	August 2010	No
NISTIR 7676	Maintaining and Using Key History on Peronal Indentity Verification (PIV) Cards	March 2010	Yes - June 2010
NISTIR 7669	Open Vulnerability Assessment Language (OVAL) Validation Program Derived Test Requirements	March 2010	No
NISTIR 7657	A Report on the Privilege (Access) Management Workshop	November 2009	Yes - March 2010
NISTIR 7628 (2nd draft)	Smart Grid Cyber Security Strategy and Requirements	February 2010	Yes - August 2010
NISTIR 7622	Piloting Supply Chain Risk Management Practices for Federal Information Systems	June 2010	No
NISTIR 7609	Cryptographic Key Management Workshop Summary	January 2009	Yes - Jan. 2010
NISTIR 7601	Framework for Emergency Response Officials (ERO) Authentication and Authorization Infrastructure	December 2009	Yes - Aug. 2010

NISTIR 7511 Revision 2	Security Content Automation Protocol (SCAP) Version 1.0 Validation Program Test Requirements	April 2010	No
NISTIR 7298 Revision 1	Glossary of Key Information Security Terms	May 2010	No
NISTIR 7275 Revision 4	Specification for the Extensible Configuration Checklist Description Format (XCCDF) Version 1.2	July 2010	No

Federal Information Processing Standards

None Released as Final in FY 2010

Special Publications

Number	Title	Date Released
SP 800-127	Guide to Securing WIMAX Wireless Communications	September 2010
SP 800-122	Guide to Protecting the Confidentiality of Peronally Indentifiable Information (PII)	April 2010
SP 800-117	Guide to Adopting and Using the Security Content Automation Protocol (SCAP) Version 1.0	July 2010
SP 800-85A-2	PIV Card Application and Middleware Interface Test Guidelines (SP800-73-3 Compliance)	July 2010
SP800-81 Revision 1	Secure Domain Name System (DNS) Deployment Guide	August 2010
SP 800-78-2	Crytographic Algorithms and Key Sizes for Personal Identification Verification (PIV)	February 2010
SP 800-73-3	Interfaces for Personal Identity Verification	February 2010
SP 800-57	Recommendation for Key Management, Part 3: Application-Specific Key Management Guidance	December 2009
SP 800-53A Revision1	Guide for Assessing the Security Controls in Federal Information Systems and Organizations	June 2010
SP 800-38E	Recommendation for Block Cipher Modes of Operation: The XTS-AES Mode for Confidentiality on Storage Devices	January 2010
Sp 800-37 Revision 1	Guide for Applying the Risk Management Framework to Federal Information Systems: A Security Life Cycle Approach	February 2010
SP 800-34 Revision 1	Contingency Planning Guide for Federal information Systems	May 2010

NIST Interagency Reports:

Publication #:	Title:	Date Released:
NISTIR 7676	Maintaining and Using Key History on Personal Identity Verification (PIV) Cards	June 2010
NISTIR 7665	Proceedings of the Privilege Management Workshop, September 1-3, 2009	March 2010
NISTIR 7658	Guide to SIMfill Use and Development	February 2010
NISTIR 7657	A Report on the Privilege (Access) Management Worshop	March 2010
NISTIR 7653	2009 Computer Security Division Annual Report	March 2010
NISTIR 7628	Guidelines for Smart Grid Cyber Security	August 2010
NISTIR 7621	Small Business Iformation Security: The Fundamentals	October 2009
NISTIR 7617	Mobile Forensic Reference Materials: A Methodology and Reification	October 2009
NISTIR 7609	Cryptographic Key Management Worshop Summary - June 8-9, 2009	January 2010

NISTIR 7601	Framework for Emergency response officials (ERO)	August 2010
NISTIR 7559	Forensics Web Services (FWS)	June 2010
NISTIR 7497	Security Architecture Design Process for Health Information Exchanges (HIE)	September 2010

ITL Security Bulletins:

Title:	Date Released:
Security Content Automation Protocol (SCAP) Helping Organizations Maintain and Verify The Security of Their Information Systems	September 2010
Assessing The Effectiveness of Security Controls in Federal Information Systems	August 2010
Contingency Planning For Information Systems: Updated Guide For Federal Organizations	July 2010
How To Identify Personnel With Significant Reponsibilities For Information Security	June 2010
Guide To Protecting Personally Identifiable Information	April 2010
Revised Guide Helps Federal Organizations Improve Their Risk Management Practices and Information System Security	March 2010
Secure Management Of Keys in Cryptographic Applications: Guidance For Organizations	February 2010
Security Metrics: Measurements To Support The Continued Development of Information Security Technology	January 2010
Crybersecurity Fundamentals For Small Business Owners	November 2009
Protecting Information Systems With Firewalls: Revised Guidelines On Firewall Technologies and Policies	October 2009

2010 Guidelines and Documents Abstracts

This section contains a short abstract of all the guidelines and documents (Special Publications and NIST Interagency Reports) released during FY2010 (October 1, 2009 to September 30, 2010). Note, the documents with "DRAFT" in the title, they were not finalized during FY2010 and remained in draft status.

Special Publications (SPs)

DRAFT SP 800-135, Recommendation for Existing Application-Specific Key Derivation Functions
Group: Cryptographic Technology

Cryptographic keys are vital to the security of internet security applications and protocols. Many widely-used internet security protocols have their own application specific Key Derivation Functions (KDFs) that are used to generate the cryptographic keys required for their cryptographic functions. This Recommendation provides security requirements for those KDFs.

Contact:
Mr. Quynh Dang
quynh.dang@nist.gov

DRAFT SP 800-132, Recommendation for Password-Based Key Derivation Part 1: Storage Applications
Group: Cryptographic Technology

The randomness of cryptographic keys is essential for the security of cryptographic applications. In some applications, such as the protection of electronically stored data, passwords may be the only input required from the users who are eligible to access the data. Due to the low entropy and possibly poor randomness of those passwords, they are not suitable to be used directly as cryptographic keys. This Recommendation specifies a family of password-based key derivation functions (PBKDFs) for deriving cryptographic keys from passwords or passphrases for the protection of electronically-stored data or for the protection of data protection keys.

Contacts:
Ms. Elaine Barker
elaine.barker@nist.gov

Mr. William Burr
william.burr@nist.gov

Dr. Lily Chen
lily.chen@nist.gov

DRAFT SP 800-131, Transitions: Recommendation for Transitioning the Use of Cryptographic Algorithms and Key Lengths
Group: Cryptographic Technology

At the start of the 21st century, the National Institute of Standards and Technology (NIST) began the task of providing cryptographic key management guidance, which includes defining and implementing appropriate key management procedures, using algorithms that adequately protect sensitive information, and planning ahead for possible changes in the use of cryptography because of algorithm breaks or the availability of more powerful computing techniques. NIST Special Publication (SP) 800-57, Part 1, Recommendation for Key Management, the first document produced in this effort, includes a general approach for transitioning from one algorithm or key length to another. This Recommendation (SP 800-131A) provides more specific guidance for transitions to the use of stronger cryptographic keys and more robust algorithms.

Contacts:
Ms. Elaine Barker
elaine.barker@nist.gov

Mr. Allen Roginsky
allen.roginsky@nist.gov

DRAFT SP 800-130, A Framework for Designing Cryptographic Key Management Systems
Group: Cryptographic Technology

This Framework for Designing Cryptographic Key Management Systems (CKMS) contains descriptions of CKMS components that should be considered by a CKMS designer and specifies requirements for the documentation of those CKMS components in the design. This Framework places documentation requirements on the CKMS design document. As a result, any CKMS, that is properly documented, could have a design document that is compliant with this Framework.

Contact:
Ms. Elaine Barker
elaine.barker@nist.gov

DRAFT SP 800-128, Guide for Security Configuration Management of Information Systems
Group: Security Management and Assurance

An information system is typically in a constant state of change in response to new or enhanced hardware and software capability, patches for correcting errors to existing components, new security threats, changing business functions, etc. Implementing information system changes almost always results in some adjustment to the system information security configuration baseline. To ensure that adjustments to the system configuration do not adversely affect the security of the information system, a well-defined security configuration management process is needed. This publication is intended to provide guidelines for organizations responsible for managing changes to security configurations of federal information system computing environments. This publication also provides supporting guidance for implementation of the Configuration Management family of security controls defined in NIST SP 800-53, Recommended Security Controls for Federal Information Systems and Organizations.

The initial draft of NIST SP 800-128 was released for public comment March 2010 and is expected to be released as a final document in FY2011.

Contact:
Mr. Arnold Johnson
(301) 975-3247
arnold.johnson@nist.gov

SP 800-127, Guide to Securing WiMAX Wireless Communications
Group: Systems and Emerging Technologies Security Research

This document provides information to organizations regarding the security capabilities of wireless communications using WiMAX networks and provides recommendations on using these capabilities. WiMAX technology is a wireless metropolitan area network (WMAN) technology based upon the IEEE 802.16 standard. It is used for a variety of purposes, including, but not limited to, fixed last-mile broadband access, long-range wireless backhaul, and access layer technology for mobile wireless subscribers operating on telecommunications networks.

Contact:
Mr. David Ferraiolo
david.ferraiolo@nist.gov

DRAFT SP 800-126 Revision 1, The Technical Specification for the Security Content Automation Protocol (SCAP): SCAP Version 1.1
Group: Systems and Emerging Technologies Security Research

This document defines the technical specification for Version 1.0 of the Security Content Automation Protocol (SCAP). SCAP consists of a suite of specifications for standardizing the format and nomenclature by which security software communicates information about software flaws and security configurations. This document describes the basics of the SCAP component specifications and their interrelationships, the characteristics of SCAP content, as well as SCAP requirements not defined in the individual SCAP component specifications. This guide provides recommendations on how to use SCAP to achieve security auto-

mation for organizations seeking to implement SCAP.

Contacts:
Mr. David Waltermire   Mr. Stephen Quinn
david.waltermire@nist.gov   stephen.quinn@nist.gov

DRAFT SP 800-125, Guide to Security for Full Virtualization Technologies
Group: Systems and Emerging Technologies Security Research

This draft SP 800-125 discusses the security concerns associated with full virtualization technologies for server and desktop virtualization, and provides recommendations for addressing these concerns. Full virtualization technologies run one or more operating systems and their applications on top of virtual hardware. Full virtualization is used for operational efficiency, such as in cloud computing, and for allowing users to run applications for multiple operating systems on a single computer.

Contact:
Mr. Murugiah Souppaya
murugiah.souppaya@nist.gov

SP 800-122, Guide to Protecting the Confidentiality of Personally Identifiable Information (PII)
Group: Systems and Emerging Technologies Security Research

This document assists Federal agencies in protecting the confidentiality of personally identifiable information (PII) in information systems. The document explains the importance of protecting the confidentiality of PII in the context of information security and explains its relationship to privacy using the Fair Information Practices, which are the principles underlying most privacy laws and privacy best practices. PII should be protected from inappropriate access, use, and disclosure. This publication provides practical, context-based guidance for identifying PII and determining what level of protection is appropriate for each instance of PII. SP800-122 also suggests safeguards that may offer appropriate levels of protection for PII and provides recommendations for developing response plans for incidents involving PII. Organizations are encouraged to tailor the recommendations to meet their specific requirements.

Contacts:
Ms. Erika McCallister   Mr. Tim Grance
erika.mccallister@nist.gov   grance@nist.gov

DRAFT SP 800-119, Guidelines for the Secure Deployment of IPv6
Group: Systems and Emerging Technologies Security Research

Due to the exhaustion of IPv4 address space, and the Office of Management and Budget (OMB) mandate that U.S. federal agencies begin to use the IPv6 protocol, NIST undertook the development of a guide to help educate federal agencies about the possible security risks during their initial IPv6 deployment. Since

IPv6 is not backwards compatible with IPv4, organizations will have to change their network infrastructure and systems to deploy IPv6. This document provides guidelines for organizations to aid in securely deploying IPv6. The goals of this document are: To educate the reader about IPv6 features and the security impacts of those features; To provide a comprehensive survey of mechanisms that can be used for the deployment of IPv6; To provide a suggested deployment strategy for moving to an IPv6 environment. The guidelines will help organizations understand the features of IPv6 and how it compares to IPv4, the security impacts of IPv6 features and capabilities, the potential impacts of IPv6 deployment, and the range of IPv4 to IPv6 transition mechanisms.

Contact:
Ms. Sheila Frankel
sheila.frankel@nist.gov

SP 800-117, Guide to Adopting and Using the Security Content Automation Protocol (SCAP) Version 1.0
Group: Systems and Emerging Technologies Security Research

This document provides an overview of the Security Content Automation Protocol (SCAP). The publication discusses SCAP at a conceptual level, focusing on how organizations can use SCAP-enabled tools to enhance their security posture. It also explains to IT product and service vendors how they can adopt SCAP's capabilities within their offerings.

Contact:
Mr. Stephen Quinn
stephen.quinn@nist.gov

SP 800-85A-2, PIV Card Application and Middleware Interface Test Guidelines (SP800-73-3 compliance)
Group: Systems and Emerging Technologies Security Research

This document provides test requirements and test assertions that can be used to validate the compliance/conformance of two PIV components: PIV middleware and PIV card application with the specification in NIST SP 800-73-3, Interfaces for Personal Identity Verification, Pt. 3- PIV Client Application Programming Interface.

Contacts:
Dr. Ramaswamy Chandramouli (Mouli)   Ms. Hildegard Ferraiolo
mouli@nist.gov   hferraiolo@nist.gov

Mr. Ketan Mehta
ketan.mehta@nist.gov

SP 800-81 Revision 1, Secure Domain Name System (DNS) Deployment Guide
Group: Systems and Emerging Technologies Security Research

This document provides deployment guidelines for securing

DNS within an enterprise. Because DNS data is meant to be public, preserving the confidentiality of DNS data pertaining to publicly accessible IT resources is not a concern. The primary security goals for DNS are data integrity and source authentication, which are needed to ensure the authenticity of domain name information and maintain the integrity of domain name information in transit. This document provides extensive guidance on maintaining data integrity and performing source authentication. Availability of DNS services and data is also very important; DNS components are often subjected to denial-of-service attacks intended to disrupt access to the resources whose domain names are handled by the attacked DNS components. This document presents guidelines for configuring DNS deployments to prevent many denial-of-service attacks that exploit vulnerabilities in various DNS components.

Contact:
Dr. Ramaswamy Chandramouli (Mouli)
mouli@nist.gov

SP 800-78-2, Cryptographic Algorithms and Key Sizes for Personal Identity Verification
Group: Cryptographic Technology

This document contains the technical specifications needed for the mandatory and optional cryptographic keys, as well as the supporting infrastructure specified in FIPS 201, Personal Identity Verification (PIV) of Federal Employees and Contractors, and the related Special Publication 800-73, Interfaces for Personal Identity Verification, and SP 800-76, Biometric Data Specification for Personal Identity Verification, that rely on cryptographic functions.

Contacts:
Mr. Tim Polk   Ms. Donna Dodson
tim.polk@nist.gov   donna.dodson@nist.gov

Mr. William Burr
william.burr@nist.gov

SP 800-73-3, Interfaces for Personal Identity Verification (4 parts):
Part 1 End-Point PIV Card Application Namespace, Data Model and Representation
Part 2 End-Point PIV Card Application Card Command Interface
Part 3 End-Point Client Application Programming Interface
Part 4 The PIV Transitional Data Model and Interfaces
Group: Systems and Emerging Technologies Security Research

FIPS 201, Personal Identity Verification (PIV) of Federal Employees and Contractors, defines procedures for the PIV lifecycle activities including identity proofing, registration, PIV Card issuance, and PIV Card usage. FIPS 201 also specifies that the identity credentials must be stored on a smart card. SP 800-73-3 contains the technical specifications to interface with the smart card to retrieve and use the identity credentials. The specifications reflect the design goals of interoperability and PIV Card functions. The goals are addressed by specifying a PIV data model, card edge interface, and application programming interface. In addition, SP 800-73-3 enumerates requirements where the standards include options and branches.

Contacts:

Dr. Ramaswamy Chandramouli
mouli@nist.gov

Mr. David Cooper
david.cooper@nist.gov

Ms. Hildegard Ferraiolo
hferraio@nist.gov

Mr. William MacGregor
william.macgregor@nist.gov

Mr. Ketan Mehta
ketan.mehta@nist.gov

SP 800-57 PART 3, Recommendation for Key Management
Group: Cryptographic Technology

Special Publication 800-57 provides cryptographic key management guidance. It consists of three parts: Part 1 provides general guidance and best practices for the management of cryptographic keying material; Part 2 provides guidance on policy and security planning requirements for U.S. government agencies; Part 3 provides guidance for using the cryptographic features of current systems.

Contacts:

Mr. Tim Polk
tim.polk@nist.gov

Ms. Elaine Barker
elaine.barker@nist.gov

Mr. Quynh Dang
Quynh.dang@nist.gov

DRAFT SP 800-56C, Recommendation for Key Derivation through Extraction-then-Expansion
Group: Cryptographic Technology

This Recommendation specifies techniques for the derivation of keying material from a shared secret established during a key establishment scheme defined in NIST Special Publications 800-56A, Recommendation for Pair-Wise Key Establishment Schemes Using Discrete Logarithm Cryptography, and 800-56B, Recommendation for Pair-Wise Key Establishment Schemes Using Integer Factorization Cryptography, through an extraction-then-expansion procedure.

Contact:

Ms. Lily Chen
lily.chen@nist.gov

SP 800-53A, Revision 1, Guide for Assessing the Security Controls in Federal Information Systems and Organizations, Building Effective Security Assessment Plans
Group: Security Management and Assurance

NIST SP 800-53A, Revision 1, is the third in the series of publications developed by the Joint Task Force Transformation Initiative. The updated security assessment guideline incorporates best practices in information security from the Department of Defense, Intelligence Community, and Civil agencies and includes security control assessment procedures for both national security and non national security systems. The guideline for developing security assessment plans is intended to support a wide variety of assessment activities in all phases of the system development life cycle including development, implementation, and operation. The important changes in SP 800-53A, Revision 1, are part of a larger strategic initiative to focus on enterprise-wide, near real-time risk management; that is, managing risks from information systems in dynamic environments of operation that can adversely affect organizational operations and assets, individuals, other organizations, and the nation. The increased flexibility in the selection of assessment methods, assessment objects, and depth and coverage attribute values empowers organizations to place the appropriate emphasis on the assessment process at every stage in the system development life cycle.

Contact:

Dr. Ron Ross
(301) 975-5390
ron.ross@nist.gov

SP 800-38E, Recommendation for Block Cipher Modes of Operation: The XTS-AES Mode for Confidentiality on Storage Devices
Group: Cryptographic Technology

This publication approves the XTS-AES mode of the Advanced Encryption Standard (AES) algorithm by reference to IEEE Std 1619-2007. An additional requirement is recommended as an option for protecting the confidentiality of data on storage devices. The mode does not provide authentication of the data or its source.

Contact:

Mr. Morris Dworkin
morris.dworkin@nist.gov

SP 800-37, Revision 1, Guide for Applying the Risk Management Framework to Federal Information Systems: A Security Life Cycle Approach
Group: Security Management and Assurance

NIST SP 800-37, Revision 1, represents the second in a series of publications being developed by the Joint Task Force Transformation Initiative. For the past three years, NIST has been working in partnership with the Office of the Director of National Intelligence, the Department of Defense, and the Committee on National Security Systems to develop a unified information security framework for the federal government and its contractors. The initial publication produced by the task force, NIST SP 800-

53, Revision 3, was historic in nature—in that it created a unified security control catalog reflecting the information security requirements of both the national security community and the non-national security community. NIST SP 800-37, Revision 1, continues the transformation by significantly changing the traditional process employed by the federal government to certify and accredit federal information systems. The revised process provides greater emphasis on: (i) building information security capabilities into information systems through the application of state-of-the-practice management, operational, and technical security controls; (ii) maintaining awareness of the security state of information systems on an ongoing basis though enhanced monitoring processes; and (iii) understanding and accepting the risk to organizational operations and assets, individuals, other organizations, and the nation arising from the use of information systems.

Contact:
Dr. Ron Ross
(301) 975-5390
ron.ross@nist.gov

SP 800-34 Revision 1, Contingency Planning Guide for Federal Information Systems
Group: Security Management and Assurance

NIST SP 800-34, Rev. 1, provides instructions, recommendations, and considerations for federal information system contingency planning. Contingency planning refers to interim measures to recover information system services after a disruption. Interim measures may include relocation of information systems and operations to an alternate site, recovery of information system functions using alternate equipment, or performance of information system functions using manual methods. This guide addresses specific contingency planning recommendations for three platform types and provides strategies and techniques common to all systems.

1. Client/server systems;
2. Telecommunications systems; and
3. Mainframe systems.

This guide defines the following seven-step contingency planning process that an organization may apply to develop and maintain a viable contingency planning program for their information systems. These seven progressive steps are designed to be integrated into each stage of the system development life cycle.

1. Develop the contingency planning policy statement;
2. Conduct the business impact analysis (BIA);
3. Identify preventive controls;
4. Create contingency strategies;
5. Develop an information system contingency plan;
6. Ensure plan testing, training, and exercises; and
7. Ensure plan maintenance.

To view SP 800-34 Revision 1, please visit the CSRC website at the following URL:
http://csrc.nist.gov/publications/PubsSPs.html#800-34

Contact:
Ms. Marianne Swanson
(301) 975-3293
marianne.swanson@nist.gov

DRAFT SP 800-16, Revision 1: Information Security Training Requirements: A Role- and Performance-Based Mode
Group: Security Management and Assurance

During FY2010, CSD made significant changes to draft SP 800-16 Revision 1, Information Security Training Requirements: A Role- and Performance-Based Model. Originally published in April 1998, SP 800-16 contains a training methodology that federal departments and agencies, as well as private sector and academic institutions, can use to develop role-based information security training material.

During FY2010, we updated the draft document, incorporating changes received during a public review and comment period in FY2009. CSD recruited members of the Federal Information Systems Security Educators' Association (FISSEA) Executive Board and select FISSEA members to form a working group to assist with the update. FISSEA is a federally focused and NIST-supported organization that has information security awareness- and training-focused expertise, strengths that CSD leverages in instances where the CSD and FISSEA missions overlap.

Related to this guideline, we continued to work with stakeholders of other federally focused information security training and workforce development initiatives. The goal is to create a multi-agency task force to assist our constituents by 1) developing a diagram that shows the interactions and relationships between the various initiatives, and 2) agreeing on a common training "standard" for use by various federal communities that currently own or manage the training and workforce development initiatives.

Coupled with these efforts is the emergence of the NIST-led National Initiative for Cybersecurity Education (NICE). Under NICE's training and workforce development element, NIST is continuing to collaborate with potential partners. Discussions have begun as to the feasibility of a federal and/or national cybersecurity training standard. SP 800-16 Revision 1 is one of the several existing federal standards and guidelines that would be used to shape an eventual federal and/or national training standard.

We expect the update of SP 800-16 Revision 1 to be completed during FY2011.

Contact:
Ms. Pat Toth
(301) 975-5140
pat.toth@nist.gov

NIST Interagency Reports (NISTIRs)

DRAFT NISTIR 7697, Common Platform Enumeration: Dictionary Specification Version 2.3
Group: Systems and Emerging Technologies Security Research

This report defines the concept of a Common Platform Enumeration (CPE) Dictionary, the rules associated with CPE Dictionary creation and management, and the data model for representing a CPE Dictionary. The CPE Dictionary Specification is a part of a stack of CPE specifications that serves to support a variety of use cases relating to IT product description and naming. An individual CPE Dictionary is a repository of IT product names, with each name in the repository identifying a unique class of IT product in the world. This specification defines the semantics of the CPE Dictionary data model. The common semantics provide a shared understanding of CPE Dictionary constructs to users from different communities of practice. This specification also defines the methodology for capturing official IT product names through an Official CPE Dictionary construct.

Contacts:
Mr. David Waltermire
david.waltermire@nist.gov

Mr. Paul Cichonski
paul.cichonski@nist.gov

DRAFT NISTIR 7696, Common Platform Enumeration : Name Matching Specification Version 2.3
Group: Systems and Emerging Technologies Security Research

Common Platform Enumeration (CPE) is a standardized method of describing and identifying classes of applications, operating systems, and hardware devices present in an enterprise's computing assets. CPE can be used as a source of information for enforcing and verifying IT management policies relating to these assets, such as vulnerability, configuration, and remediation policies. IT management tools can collect information about installed products, identify products using their CPE names, and use this standardized information to help make fully or partially automated decisions regarding the assets.

This report defines the Common Platform Enumeration (CPE) Name Matching version 2.3 specification. The CPE Name Matching specification is part of a stack of CPE specifications that support a variety of use cases relating to IT product description and naming. The CPE Name Matching specification provides a method for conducting a one-to-one comparison of a source CPE name to a target CPE name. In addition to defining the specification, this report also defines and explains the requirements that IT products must meet for conformance with the CPE Name Matching version 2.3 specification.

Contacts:
Mr. David Waltermire
david.waltermire@nist.gov

Mr. Harold Booth
harold.booth@nist.gov

DRAFT NISTIR 7695, Common Platform Enumeration: Naming Specification Version 2.3
Group: Systems and Emerging Technologies Security Research

This report defines the Common Platform Enumeration (CPE) Naming version 2.3 specification. The CPE Naming specification is a part of a stack of CPE specifications that support a variety of use cases relating to IT product description and naming. The CPE Naming specification defines the logical structure of names for IT product classes and the procedures for binding and unbinding these names to and from machine-readable encodings. This report also defines and explains the requirements that IT products must meet for conformance with the CPE Naming version 2.3 specification.

The CPE stack includes the Naming specification defined in draft NISTIR 7695; the Name Matching specification defined in draft NISTIR 7696; the Dictionary specification, which defines the concept of a dictionary of identifiers and prescribes high-level rules for dictionary curators; and the Language specification which defines an approach for forming complex logical expressions out of well-formed CPE names (WFNs).

Contact:
Mr. David Waltermire
david.waltermire@nist.gov

NISTIR 7676, Maintaining and Using Key History on Personal Identity Verification (PIV) Cards
Group: Cryptographic Technology

NIST Special Publication 800-73-3, Interfaces for Personal Identity Verification – Part 1: End-Point PIV Card Application Namespace, Data Model and Representation, discusses methods for storing retired Key Management Keys within the Personal Identity Verification (PIV) Card Application on a PIV Card. NISTIR 7676 complements SP 800-73-3 by providing some of the rationale for the design of the mechanism for storing retired Key Management Keys on PIV Cards and by providing suggestions to smart card vendors, PIV Card Issuers, and middleware developers on the use of the Key History mechanism.

Contact:
Mr. David Cooper
david.cooper@nist.gov

DRAFT NISTIR 7669, Open Vulnerability Assessment Language (OVAL) Validation Program Derived Test Requirements
Group: Systems and Emerging Technologies Security Research

This report defines the requirements and associated test procedures necessary for products to achieve one or more Open Vulnerability and Assessment Language (OVAL) Validations. Validation is awarded based on testing a defined set of OVAL capabilities by independent laboratories that have been accredited for OVAL testing by the NIST National Voluntary Laboratory Accreation Program (NVLAP).

Contacts:

Mr. David Waltermire	Mr. John Banghart
david.waltermire@nist.gov	john.banghart@nist.gov

Mr. Stephen Quinn
stephen.quinn@nist.gov

NISTIR 7665, Proceedings of the Privilege Management Workshop, September 1-3, 2009
Group: Systems and Emerging Technologies Security Research

Privilege management is large and complex, often the source of heated debate and opinion, and fraught with widely-understood, yet ill-defined terminology and concepts. The National Institute of Standards and Technology (NIST) and the National Security Agency (NSA) sponsored the first Privilege Management Workshop at NIST s main campus in Gaithersburg, Maryland, September 1-3, 2009. The workshop was attended by approximately 120 people representing Executive branch federal agencies, the private sector, and academia. The primary goal of this first workshop was to bring together a wide spectrum of individuals representing differing viewpoints, use cases, and organizational needs with the intent of reaching a common understanding of several facets of this important area. This includes reaching consensus on the definition of privilege management and other terminology; understanding and analyzing the strengths and weaknesses of current and proposed access control models; ascertaining the current state of the practice and future research directions in privilege management; and understanding and articulating the managerial, legal, and policy requirements associated with privilege management.

Contacts:

Ms. Tanya Brewer	Ms. Annie Sokol
tanya.brewer@nist.gov	annie.sokol@nist.gov

NISTIR 7658, Guide to SIMfill Use and Development
Group: Systems and Emerging Technologies Security Research

SIMfill is a proof-of-concept, open source, application developed by NIST to populate identity modules with test data, as a way to assess the recovery capability of mobile forensic tools. An initial set of test data is also provided with SIMfill as a baseline for creating other test cases. This report describes the design and organization of SIMfill in sufficient detail to allow informed use and experimentation with the software and test data provided, including the option to modify and extend the program and data provided to meet specific needs.

Contact:
Mr. Wayne Jansen
wjansen@nist.gov

NISTIR 7657, A Report on the Privilege (Access) Management Workshop
Group: Systems and Emerging Technologies Security Research

This document is based on the discussions and conclusions of the Privilege (Access) Management Workshop held on 1-3 September 2009 at the Gaithersburg, Maryland facilities of the National Institute of Standards and Technology (NIST), sponsored by NIST and the National Security Agency (NSA). This document includes additional material resulting from in relevant comments made by workshop participants and the public during the review periods for this document. An overview of the workshop is available in the published proceedings of the workshop.

Contact:
Ms. Annie Sokol
annie.sokol@nist.gov

NISTIR 7653, 2009 Computer Security Division Annual Report
Group: Security Management and Assurance

This NISTIR is the 2009 Annual Report for the Computer Security Division. This report provides the highlights of the projects that the CSD carried out during FY2009.

Contacts:

Mr. Patrick O'Reilly	Mr. Matthew Scholl
patrick.oreilly@nist.gov	matthew.scholl@nist.gov

NISTIR 7628, Guidelines for Smart Grid Cyber Security
Group: Security Management and Assurance

Smart Grid technologies will introduce millions of new intelligent components to the electric grid and will enable more advanced communications (e.g., two-way communications, and wired and wireless communications) than was possible in the past. This report assists individuals and organizations who will be addressing cyber security for Smart Grid systems. The privacy recommendations, the security requirements, and the supporting analyses that are included in this report may be used by strategists, designers, implementers, and operators of the Smart Grid, e.g., utilities, equipment manufacturers, regulators, as input to their risk assessment process and other tasks in the security lifecycle of a Smart Grid information system. This report focuses on specifying an analytical framework that may be useful to an organization. It is a baseline, and each organization must develop its own cyber security strategy for the Smart Grid. The information in this report provides guidance to organizations in assessing risk and selecting appropriate security requirements and privacy recommendations.

Contacts:

Ms. Marianne Swanson	Ms. Tanya Brewer
marianne.swanson@nist.gov	tanya.brewer@nist.gov

Ms. Annabelle Lee

DRAFT NISTIR 7622, Piloting Supply Chain Risk Management Practices for Federal Information Systems
Group: Security Management and Assurance

This document provides a set of practices that can be referenced or used for those information systems categorized at the FIPS (Federal Information Processing Standards) 199 high-impact level. Organizations determine the security category of their information system in accordance with FIPS 199, Standards for Security Categorization of Federal Information and Information Systems and then derive the information system impact level from the security category in accordance with FIPS 200, Minimum Security Requirements for Federal Information and Information Systems. The practices discussed in the draft publication help to promote the acquisition, development, and operation of information systems or system-of-systems that meet cost, schedule, and performance requirements in today's environment with globalized suppliers and active adversaries. When integrated within the information systems development life cycle (SDLC), these practices provide risk mitigating strategies for federal agencies to implement.

Contact:
Ms. Marianne Swanson
marianne.swanson@nist.gov

NISTIR 7621, Small Business Information Security: The Fundamentals
Group: Security Management and Assurance

NIST, in partnership with the Small Business Administration and the Federal Bureau of Investigation has had educational outreach to the small business community since 2002. With full participation from our partners, we schedule, promote, and conduct information security workshops for small businesses throughout the United States.

The core information in the workshops has been collected in NISTIR 7621, Small Business Information Security: The Fundamentals. This document covers the fundamentals of information security for small business. The intent was to publish a short, easy to read document that small business owners could use to protect the information, computers, and networks used in their small businesses.

The draft of NISTIR 7621 was released for public comment in September 2009 and was planned for release as a final document in the first quarter of FY2010.

NISTIR 7621 was released as a final document in October 2009 (FY2010/Q1).

Contact:
Mr. Richard Kissel
richard.kissel@nist.gov

NISTIR 7617, Mobile Forensic Reference Materials: A Methodology and Reification
Group: Systems and Emerging Technologies Security Research

This report is about the theoretical and practical issues associated with automatically populating mobile devices with reference test data for use as reference materials in validation of forensic tools. NISTIR 7617 describes an application and data set developed to populate identity modules and highlights subtleties involved in the process. Intriguing results attained by recent versions of commonly-used forensic tools when used to recover the populated data are also discussed. The results indicate that reference materials can be used to identify a variety of inaccuracies that exist in present-day forensic tools.

Contact:
Mr. Wayne Jansen
wjansen@nist.gov

NISTIR 7609, Cryptographic Key Management Workshop Summary
Group: Cryptographic Technology

On June 8 and 9, 2009, NIST held a Cryptographic Key Management (CKM) Workshop at its Gaithersburg, Maryland, campus. This summary provides the highlights of workshop presentations organized both by major CKM topics and by presenters.

Contact:
Ms. Elaine Barker
elaine.barker@nist.gov

NISTIR 7601, Framework for Emergency Response Officials (ERO)
Group: Systems and Emerging Technologies Security Research

This document describe a framework (with the acronym ERO-AA) for establishing an infrastructure for authentication and authorization of Emergency Response officials (ERO) who respond to various types of human-made and natural disasters. The population of individuals authenticated and authorized under ERO-AA infrastructure includes Federal Emergency Response Officials (FEROs), State/Local/Tribal/Private Sector Emergency Response Officials (SLTP-EROs) and the FEMA Disaster Reserve Workforce (DRW). The system supports the establishment, conveyance and validation of Identity Credentials (ICs), Attribute Credentials (ATs) and Deployment Authorization Credentials (DAs). Apart from enumeration of the types of EROs and their associated authority domains (called major players) and types of credentials, the conceptualization of the framework for ERO-AA infrastructure includes detailed description of various component services under three major service classes: Credentialing Service Class, Identity Verification and Attribute Validation Service Class and Trust Federation Service Class. The framework is predicated upon the use of trusted tokens capable of supporting biometric as well as secret key based identity authentication.

Contacts:

Dr. Ramaswamy Chandramouli   Ms.Teresa Schwarzhoff
mouli@nist.gov   teresa.schwarzhoff@nist.gov

NISTIR 7559, Forensics Web Services (FWS)
Group: Systems and Emerging Technologies Security Research

Web services are currently a preferred way to develop and provide complex services. This complexity arises due to the composition of new services and dynamically invoking existing services. These compositions create service inter-dependencies that can be misused for monetary or other gains. When a misuse is reported, investigators have to navigate through a collection of logs to recreate the attack. In order to facilitate that task, the report proposes creating forensics web services (FWS) that would securely maintain transactional records between other web services. These secure records can be re-linked to reproduce the transactional history by an independent agency. The report demonstrates the necessary components of a forensic framework for web services and its success through a case study.

Contact:
Dr. Anoop Singhal
anoop.singhal@nist.gov

DRAFT NISTIR 7511 Revision 2, Security Content Automation Protocol (SCAP) Version 1.0 Validation Program Test Requirements
Group: Systems and Emerging Technologies Security Research

This report defines the requirements and associated test procedures necessary for products to achieve one or more Security Content Automation Protocol (SCAP) validations. Validation is awarded based on a defined set of SCAP capabilities by independent laboratories that have been accredited for SCAP testing by the NIST National Voluntary Laboratory Accreditation Program (NVLAP).

Contacts:

Mr. David Waltermire   Mr. John Banghart
david.waltermire@nist.gov   john.banghart@nist.gov

Mr. Stephen Quinn
Stephen.quinn@nist.gov

NISTIR 7497, Security Architecture Design Process for Health Information Exchanges (HIEs)
Group: Security Management and Assurance

This publication provides a systematic approach to designing a technical security architecture for the exchange of health information that leverages common government and commercial practices and that demonstrates how these practices can be applied to the development of HIEs. This publication assists organizations in ensuring that data protection is adequately addressed throughout the system development life cycle, and that these data protection mechanisms are applied when the organization develops technologies that enable the exchange of health information.

Contacts:

Mr. Kevin Stine   Mr. Matthew Scholl
kevin.stine@nist.gov   matthew.scholl@nist.gov

DRAFT NISTIR 7298, Revision 1, Glossary of Key Information Security Terms
Group: Security Management and Assurance

Over the years, CSD has produced many information security guidance documents with definitions of key terms used. However, the definition for any given term was not standardized; therefore, there were multiple definitions for a given term. In 2004, CSD identified a need to increase consistency in definitions for key information security terms in our documents.

The first step was a review of NIST publications (NISTIRs, SPs, and FIPS) to determine how key information security terms were defined in each document. This review was completed in 2005 and resulted in a listing of each term and all definitions for each term. Several rounds of internal and external reviews were completed, and comments and suggestions were incorporated into the document. The document was published in April 2006 as NISTIR 7298, Glossary of Key Information Security Terms.

In 2007, CSD initiated an update to the Glossary to reflect new terms and any different definitions used in our publications, as well as to incorporate those information assurance terms from the Committee on National Security Systems Instruction No 4009 (CNSSI-4009). The glossary update was well underway when CSD was notified that CNSSI-4009 was being updated. NIST obtained a position on the CNSSI-4009 Glossary Working Group and has been working on that project since early 2008.

The updated draft NIST glossary was released for public comment in FY2010 and includes all terms and definitions in the updated CNSSI-4009.

The CSD-internal and external reviewers of the document suggested that the Glossary incorporate all new SPs released since the public draft was released in FY2010. This will delay the release of NISTIR 7298 Revision 1 to the early part of FY2011.

Contact:
Mr. Richard Kissel
(301) 975-5017
richard.kissel@nist.gov

DRAFT NISTIR 7275 Revision 4, Specification for the Extensible Configuration Checklist Description Format (XCCDF) Version 1.2

Group: Systems and Emerging Technologies Security Research

This report specifies the data model and Extensible Markup Language (XML) representation for the Extensible Configuration Checklist Description Format (XCCDF) Version 1.2. An XCCDF document is a structured collection of security configuration rules for some set of target systems. The XCCDF specification is designed to support information interchange, document generation, organizational and situational tailoring, automated compliance testing, and compliance scoring. The specification also defines a data model and format for storing results of security guidance or checklist compliance testing. XCCDF provides a uniform foundation for expression of security checklists and other configuration guidance, and thereby fosters more widespread application of good security practices.

Contact:
Mr. David Waltermire
david.waltermire@nist.gov

Ways To Engage Our Division And NIST

Guest Research Internships at NIST

Opportunities are available at NIST for 6- to 24-month internships within CSD. Qualified individuals should contact CSD, provide a statement of qualifications, and indicate the area of work that is of interest. Generally speaking, the salary costs are borne by the sponsoring institution; however, in some cases, these guest research internships carry a small monthly stipend paid by NIST. For further information, contact Ms. Donna Dodson, (301) 975-3669, donna.dodson@nist.gov or Mr. Matthew Scholl, (301) 975-2941, matthew.scholl@nist.gov.

Details at NIST for Government or Military Personnel

Opportunities are available at NIST for 6- to 24-month details at NIST in CSD. Qualified individuals should contact CSD, provide a statement of qualifications, and indicate the area of work that is of interest. Generally speaking, the salary costs are borne by the sponsoring agency; however, in some cases, agency salary costs may be reimbursed by NIST. For further information, contact Ms. Donna Dodson, (301) 975-3669, donna.dodson@nist.gov or Mr. Matthew Scholl, (301) 975-2941, matthew.scholl@nist.gov.

Federal Computer Security Program Managers' Forum

The FCSPM Forum is covered in detail in the Outreach section of this report. Membership is free and open to federal employees. For further information, contact Mr. Kevin Stine, (301) 975-4483, kevin.stine@nist.gov or visit the FCSPM Forum website at http://csrc.nist.gov/groups/SMA/forum/membership.html

Security Research

NIST occasionally undertakes security work, primarily in the area of research, funded by other agencies. Such sponsored work is accepted by NIST when it can cost-effectively further the goals of NIST and the sponsoring institution. For further information, contact Donna Dodson, Chief, Computer Security Division, donna.dodson@nist.gov

Funding Opportunities at NIST

NIST funds indusrial and academic research in a variety of ways. Our Technology Innovation Program provides cost-shared awards to industry, universities, and consortia for research on poten-tially revolutionary technologies that address critical national and societal needs in NIST's areas of technical competence, see http://www.nist.gov/tip. The Small Business Innovation Research Program funds R&D proposals from small businesses see www.nist.gov/sbir. We also offer other grants to encourage work in specific fields: precision measurement, fire research, and materials science. Grants/awards supporting research at industry, academia, and other institutions are available on a competitive basis through several different Institute offices.

For general information on NIST grants programs, please contact Christopher Hunton at christopher.hunton@nist.gov and (301) 975-5718. Further details on funding opportunities may be found on http://www.nist.gov/director/ocfo/grants/grants.cfm.

Summer Undergraduate Research Fellowship (SURF)

Curious about physics, electronics, manufacturing, chemistry, materials science, or structural engineering? Intrigued by nanotechnology, fire research, information technology, or robotics? Tickled by biotechnology or biometrics? Have an intellectual fancy for superconductors or perhaps semiconductors?

Here's your chance to satisfy that curiosity, by spending part of your summer working elbow-to-elbow with researchers at NIST, one of the world's leading research organizations and home to three Nobel Prize winners. Gain valuable hands-on experience, work with cutting-edge technology, and sample the Washington, D.C., area. And get paid while you're learning. Applications must be submitted by an academic institution (e.g., by the chair of an academic department or by appropriate administrative staff).

SURF is a partnership, supported by NIST, NSF, and the participating colleges and universities. Additional information on student eligibility criteria, plan of operation, and contacts can be found through the website http://www.nist.gov/itl/itl-surf-program.cfm or contact NIST SURF Program, 100 Bureau Drive, Stop 8400, Gaithersburg, MD 20899-8499.

ACKNOWLEDGEMENTS

The editor, Patrick O'Reilly of the National Institute of Standards and Technology (NIST), wishes to thank his colleagues in the Computer Security Division, who provided write-ups on their 2009 project highlights for this annual report. The editor would also like to acknowledge Shirley Radack, Suzanne Lightman, Kevin Stine and Peggy Himes (NIST) for reviewing and providing feedback for this annual report.

Department of Commerce Emblem

U.S. Department of Commerce
Gary Locke, Secretary

National Institute of Standards and Technology
Patrick Gallagher, Director

NISTIR 7751

2010 Computer Security Division Annual Report
May 2011

Patrick O'Reilly, Editor

Visual Communications & Distribution Division (NIST)